CONTENTS

A Mathematical Genius

SRINIVASA RAMANUJAN

"Swayambhu"

**The mathematician who left indelible footprints in the Mathematical world in a short life span of 32 years, 4 months and 4 days
(22 December 1887 – 26 April 1920)**

Dr. K. Srinivasa Rao, FNASc., FTNASc.,
Senior Professor (Retd.)

The Institute of Mathematical Sciences, Chennai-600113.
Distinguished DST-Ramanujan Professor (Retd.),
Srinivasa Ramanujan Center, SASTRA University, Kumbakonam.
Director, Srinivasa Ramanujan Academy of Maths Talent,
90/1, Second Main Road, Gandhi Nagar, Adyar, Chennai 600020,
Tamilnadu, India.

Published by Zorba Books, April 2025
Website: www.zorbabooks.com
Email: info@zorbabooks.com
Author Name: Dr. K. Srinivasa Rao
Copyright ©: Dr. K. Srinivasa Rao

Title: A Mathematical Genius: Srinivasa Ramanujan

Printbook ISBN: 978-93-5896-151-5
Ebook ISBN: 978-93-5896-994-8

The publisher under the guidance and direction of the author has published the contents in this book, and the publisher takes no responsibility for the contents, its accuracy, completeness, any inconsistencies, or the statements made. The contents of the book do not reflect the opinion of the publisher or the editor. The publisher and editor shall not be liable for any errors, omissions, or the reliability of the contents of the book.

Any perceived slight against any person/s, place or organization is purely unintentional.

Zorba Books Pvt. Ltd. (opc)
Sùshant Arcade,
Next to Courtyard Marriot,
Sushant Lok 1, Gurgaon – 122009, India

Printed in India

FOREWORD

Srinivasa Ramanujan is undoubtedly a prodigious mathematician who has blazed a meteoric trail in the mathematical firmament during a short life span of 32 years, 4 months and 4 days. Most approrpriately the Prime Minister of India has declared this year as the 2012 Year of Mathematics in honour of this mathematical genius, whose 125th anniversary is being celebrated the world-over.

Many biographies have been written and perhaps the first one of these is by Dr. S. R. Ranganathan – the distinguished Librarian of the University of Madras, who was entrusted with the original Notebooks of Ramanujan by Prof. G.H. Hardy, with the statement that Ramanujan 'is your countryman' and the Notebooks therefore 'belong to your country'. Dr. Ranganathan not only wrote a book: "Ramanujan: the man and the mathematician" (Asia Pub. House, 1967) but also had a role to play in the preservation of the Notebooks of Ramanujan, when he called on Pundit Jawaharlal Nehru along with Dr. K.S. Krishnan (a neighbour of Nehru in Allahabad) and Dr. Homi J. Bhabha, by getting a facsimile edition of the Notebooks brought out by the Tata Institute of Fundamanetal Research.

Dr. K. Srinivasa Rao is known to me from 1970s when he made frequent visits to Bombay as a user of the CDC 3600-160A computer at the Tata Institute of Fundamental Research. I have been a witness to his enthusiasm and passion for whatever he takes up, be it research work or popularization through his writings and lectures. I am happy that I had a role to play in inducing him to set up the PIE Pavilion at the 86th Indian Science Congress Exhibition in 1999, in Chennai, which has since become a permanent Ramanujan Gallery at the Periyar Science and Technology Centre and recently enlarged into a full-fledged Ramanujan Mathematics Museum. I had the pleasure and privilege of encouraging him to produce two CD ROMs on the Life and Work of Ramanujan, in 2005, at the conclusion of 2 and ½ year of efforts with his design of the contents and their production was by the National Multimedia Resource Center, Pune, with financial support from the Department of Science and Technology and their dissemination entrusted to Vigyan Prasar.

Srinivasa Rao wrote his first book on Ramanujan in 1998, which was revised in 2004. He has translated the book in Tamil written by T. V. Rangaswamy ('Ragami') entitled "Ganithamedhai Ramanujan" into English in 2008. In this the 125th Year of Ramanujan's birth, I am happy that he is coming out with a shorter student edition of the life and work of Ramanujan which I hope will become popular as a first introduction to the life and work of Ramanujan. I am happy to recommend this book strongly to students of mathematics and the general public.

– Dr. V.S. Ramamurthy

Bangalore, Aug.201 Director,
National Inst. for Advamced Study.

K.V. Rangaswami
Advisor to the Chairman

1ˢᵗ October' 2012

FOREWORD

With India's aspiration to join the league of developed nations, two things cannot be ignored viz. 1. Focus on basic Research, 2. Technological Development. Be it any field ranging from Agriculture to Aerospace, Mining to Medical, Defence to Disaster Management, Infrastructure to Information Technology, Retail to Real Estate, Automobiles to Oil Exploration – all of them thrive mainly on Engineering and Technological development. Needless to mention that Mathematics is fundamental to any stream of engineering. Therefore it is essential that students at a very young age needs to be encouraged to develop interest in Mathematics. I am sure that this book by far will meet that requirement.

My sincere compliments to Dr. K. Srinivasa Rao for devoting his time to do an in-depth research into the chronicles of the legendary mathematician Shri. Srinivasa Ramanujan. While the book delves deep into some of the phenomenal works in mathematics by Shri. Ramanujan, it makes a lucid reading as well for those who may not be much interested in number-crunching. Dr. Rao and the Srinivasa Ramanujan Academy of Maths Talent, Chennai deserve rich appreciation for this wonderful initiative. I truly believe that such initiative will sow seeds in the minds of thousands of Young Indians to pursue career in Research.

The book and the life of Shri. Ramanujan becomes real-life example to the famous quote 'Follow your Passion and the Success will follow you'. Though Sri. Ramanujan didn't get much of materialistic success in his life time he is fondly remembered by millions of Indians and maths enthusiasts across the world transcending generations.

We at Larsen & Toubro believe in ethical values, performance culture and being a responsible citizen - ingrained by our founding fathers. The motto 'In Service Lies Success' and 'Customer is King' are the fire that still ignites professionals in this organization, making L&T constantly surge ahead in the areas of Engineering & Construction. In the 75th Year of L&T, we take immense pride in playing a small but meaningful role in supporting this publication. We believe that this work is bound to give greater results and impetus to the student community, not only in India but across the world.

K V Rangaswami
Advisor to Chairman – Larsen & Toubro Limited
Former Member Board and President [Construction] L&T
Chennai

Larsen & Toubro Limited
Mount Poonamallee Road, Manapakkam, P.B. No. 979, Chennai - 600 089, INDIA
Tel: +91-44-2252 6000, 2252 8000 Dir: +91-44-2252 6100 Res: +91-44-2644 3422 Fax: +91-44-2252 6990
Email: kvr@Lntecc.com www.Lntecc.com

CHAPTER I

Ramanujan was born to Komalathammal, at her parental home in Erode, on a Thursday, December 22, 1887. K. Srinivasa Iyengar, his father, was a clerk, 'gumastha', to a cloth merchant, in Kumbakonam.

Saint Ramanuja worshipped in the Vaishnavite temples.
(1017 – 1137 A.D. believed to have lived for 120 years).

The Vaishnavite saint Ramanujachariar was born on a Thursday and the name Ramanujan was the obvious choice because he was also born on a Thursday. A South Indian naming convention is to have the name of the father as an initial for all his children. The full name of the first son born to K. Srinivasa Iyengar and Komalathammal was Srinivasa Ramanujan and S. Ramanujan, was used in all his publications in the national and international journals of repute.

A plaque which adorns most temples and homes of the followers of Vaishnava philosophy depicts, Garuda (Eagle), Chakra (wheel), Thengalai (caste) mark, Conch and Hanuman.

The traditional 'akshrabhyasam' -- teaching of the 3 R's (Reading, wRiting and aRithmatic) -- for Ramanujan, was done on the Vijayadasami day, October 1, 1892, a Saturday, at Kanchipuram, a South Indian Temple City, about two hours by road from the city of Madras (Chennai).

Goddess Namagiri of Namakkal

Mother Komalathammal
(There is no photograph of the father, Kuppuswamy Srinivasa Iyengar)

Kanchipuram Temple

Ramanujan's residence, (Ramanujan's Aksharabhyas) Sarangapani Sannidhi Street, Kumbakonam)

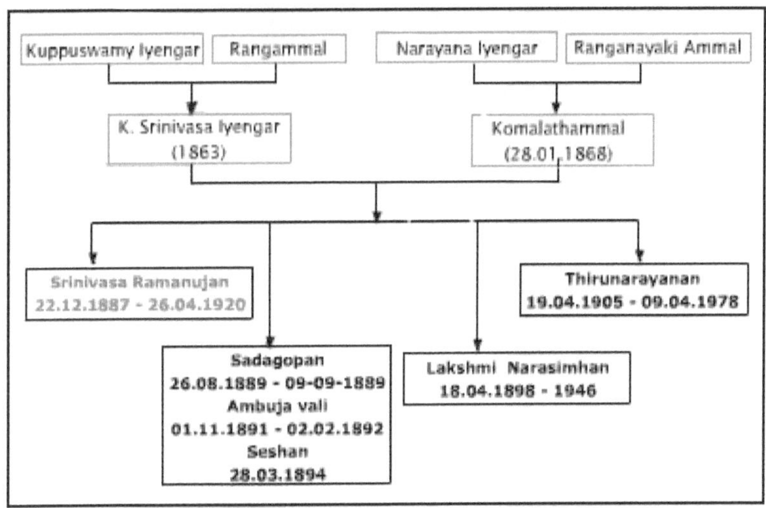

Family tree of Srinivasa Ramanujan. Note that the three births and deaths during Ramanujan's childhood would have contributed to a traumatic period for the entire family and financially difficult for the parents, in particular.

During his school days, he impressed his classmates, senior students and teachers with his extraordinary intuition and astounding proficiency in several branches of mathematics – viz. arithmetic, algebra, geometry, number theory and trigonometry. In later years, a friend of his, K. S. Viswanatha Sastri, recounted the following incident: In an arithmetic class on division, the teacher said that if three bananas were given to three students each would get one banana. The teacher generalized this idea to say that n divided by n is equal to 1. Ramanujan is said to have raised the question: "Sir, if no banana is distributed to no student, will everyone still get a banana ?"

Town High School, Kumbakonam, whose centenary was celebrated on September 20, 1964.

This authentic anecdote is one which reveals that Ramanujan was precocious and he perhaps wanted the teacher to state that:

$$n \div n = 1, \text{ for } n > 0.$$

Another classmate, K.S. Viswanatha Sastri, a lawyer, who took private tuition from Ramanujan, recalled in his article, "Reminiscences of my esteemed teacher" (in 'Ramanujan: Letters and Reminiscences', edited by P.K. Srinivasan, The Muthialpet

High School, Number Friends Society, Old Boys' Committee, Madras - 1, 1968), that:

"The one notable feature about Ramanujan was that for him pursuit of mathematics was a pursuit after God. He very often used to say that in mathematics alone, one can have a concrete realization of God. '0 ÷ 0' he used to ask 'what is its value ?' His answer was 'It may be anything. The zero of the numerator may be several times the zero of the denominator and vice versa. The value cannot be determined.' In the same way, $2^n -1$ will denote the primordial God and several identities. When n is zero the expression denotes zero, there is nothing; when n is 1, the expression denoted unity, the Infinite God; when n is 2, the expression denoted the Trinity; when n is 3, the expression denotes 7, the Saptha Rishis and so on . Another peculiarity with him was that he was extremely supple and quick in the multiplication of figures."

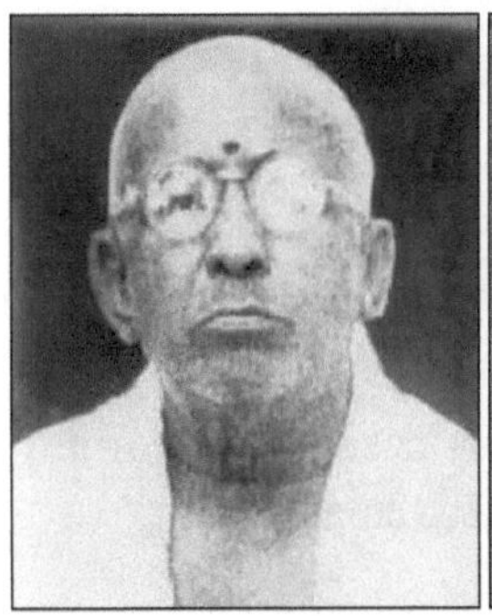

K.S. Viswanatha Sastri had tuition in mathematics from Ramanujan.　　　*S. Thirunaranan Younger brother of Ramanujan.*　　　*Smt. Rukminiammal friend of mother Komalathammal.*

Ramanujan would go to the residence of this student in Soliappa Mudali Street, every morning, and received about Rs. 7 per month as tuition fee. In his article about his tutor, he wrote:

"He was not like any ordinary tutor going step-by-step but being precocious, he would carry me off to the regions of Calculus and show me the dizzy heights to which his mind flew. ...

"He was well known among the student population, was ever resorted to by them during the examination period. He would be instructing the students on the sand of the Cauvery in solving problems likely to appear in the examination. ...

"Ramanujan had a peculiar gift of foretelling. Whenever we asked him about the possibility of a thing coming about, he would patiently hear our narration and say the answer the next day or so. He could tell us as to what would happen after dreaming of it and interpreting his dream. His interpretations mostly, proved true."

Everyday, Kamalathammal would go to the Sarangapani Temple and take part in the group singing of 'Naalaayira DIvayaprabandham', in a group led by Srimathi Rukmini Ammal. Komalathammal could recite 1000 of this 4000 verse treatise, composed by the 12 Azhwars, in praise of Lord Maha Vishnu.

Ramanujan was in the Form IV and because of his reputation, a Form VI student wanted the following question to be asked of Ramanujan, to whom neither square roots nor simultaneous equations were taught or introduced by his mathematics teachers (as these concepts were a part of Form VI syllabus), to test his precocity and to prove that Ramanujan was precocious and was very good in mathematics !

This test, in the form of a question, was posed by a Form V senior school student, C.V. Rajagopalachari to Ramanujan:

"If $\sqrt{x} + y = 7$ and $x + \sqrt{y} = 11$, what are x and y ?"

Ramanujan's immediate reply that: $x = 9$ and $y = 4$, won for him a life-long friend, who, in later years, took Ramanujan, his junior classmate and friend, to meet the Collector of Nellore, Dewan Bahadur Ramachandra Rao.

Ganapathy Subbier, the senior mathematics teacher of the school was entrusted with the responsibility of providing for the whole school conflict-free time tables. The school had about 1400 students, with an average of about 35-40 students per class. The teacher had such confidence in Ramanujan's ability that he entrusted

Ramanujan with the task of preparing the time tables for the entire school.

One may conjecture that this is possibly the time when Ramanujan started writing down diligently mathematical results as Entries in his Notebooks. For, he first chapter of his first Notebook, the only chapter in his two Notebooks which has a title, 'Magic Squares'. This chapter stands apart from the quality of the rest of the Notebooks,

since the topic of magic squares belongs to the realm of recreational mathematics. Ramanujan won prizes in his second, fourth and sixth Forms for proficiency in Mathematics and English, 'as a reward of merit and an incentive for further improvement'.

Special prize for proficiency in mathematics awarded to Ramanujan (1903).

All other chapters in his Notebooks have no titles and contain theorems in mathematics for which generations of mathematicians have tried, and are continuing to try to provide a proof, for each one of the 3254 Entries made by Ramanujan.

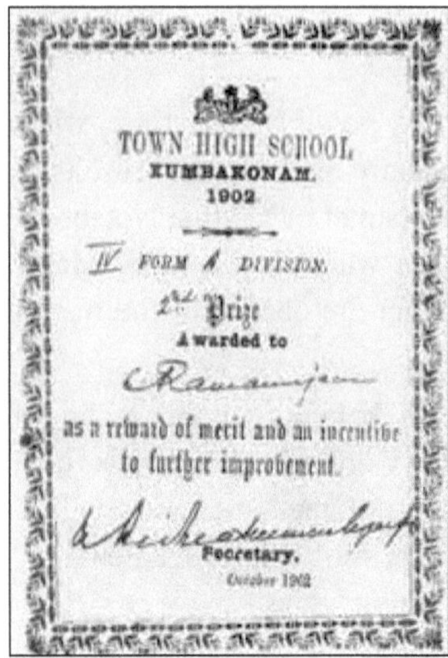

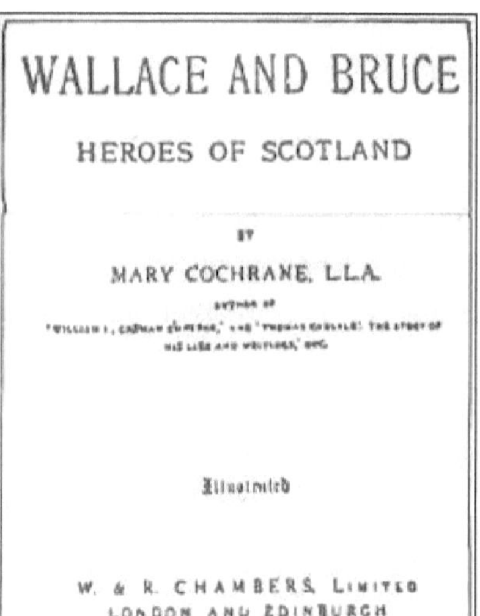

Sri Sarangapani Temple, Kumbakonam
(photo of the Raja Gopuram by author, 2002).

The house where Ramanujan lived, after it was acquired and renovated by SASTRA University, was dedicated to the Nation as a Museum, by Dr. A.P.J. Abdul Kalam, the President of India, in the year 2002.

Below, a recent photograph of the Town High School, Kumbakonam.

The Porter Hall, Kumbakonam, where Ramanujan received his public recognition.

Sarangapani Temple, Kumbakonam and the Mahamagam tank.

Chapter 2

Special prize for proficiency in mathematics awarded to Ramanujan (1903).

All other chapters in his Notebooks have no titles and contain theorems in mathematics for which generations of mathematicians have tried, and are continuing to try to provide a proof, for each one of the 3254 Entries made by Ramanujan.

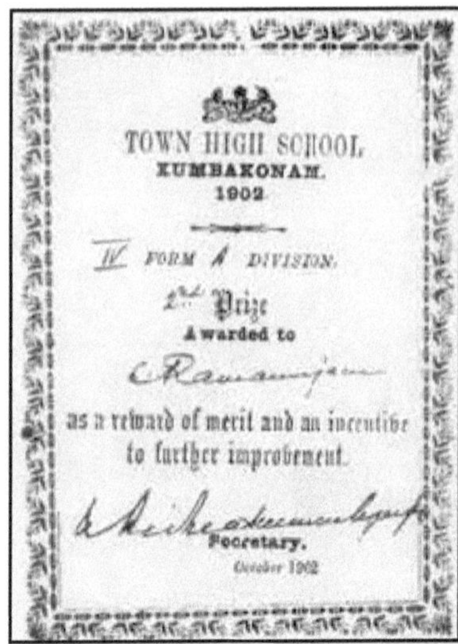

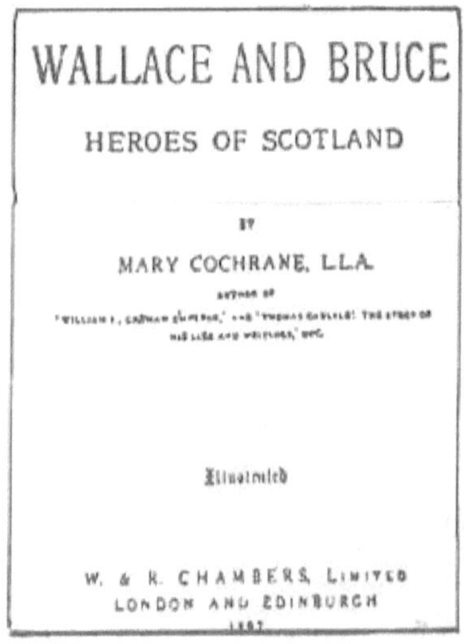

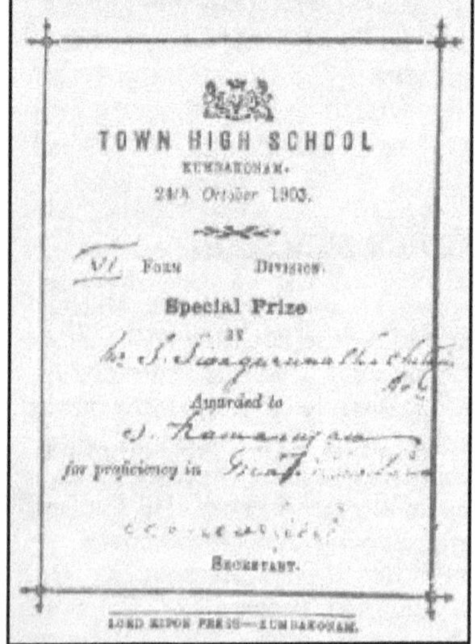

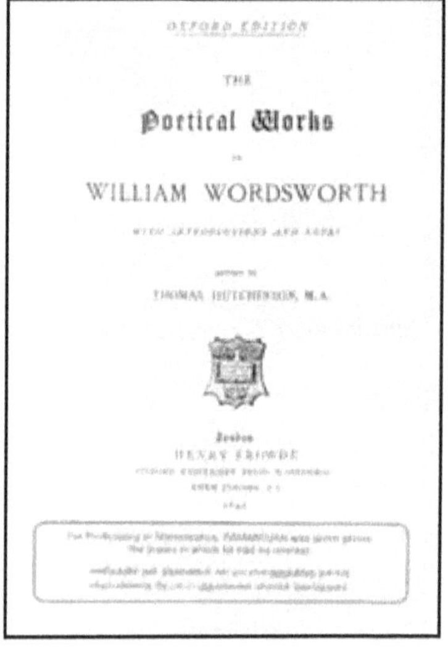

The books received by Ramanujan for proficiency in English and Mathematics, included, S.L. Loney's 'Trigono-metry'. Surprisingly, the Poetical works of William Wordsworth was given to him as a prize for his proficiency in mathematics, unlike the noteworthy efforts of the teacher of Gauss who secured a book of mathematics (from Berlin) to give it as a gift to his talented student.

To augment the family's income, Komalathammal took in a couple of students from Tirunelveli and Tiruchirapalli as boarders. Noticing the precocious nature of Ramanujan, who would reveal his insights to these senior students in casual conversations and even provide them newer, unconventional, simpler proofs for their collegiate mathematics theorems. When they told their college professors about these proofs, the teachers evoked genuine surprise and appreciation of the extraordinary talent of Ramanujan. The students in turn, gave Ramanujan an elementary introduction to the mathematics they were learning at that time.

It is through these friends studying in the Government (Arts) College, Kumbakonam that Ramanujan obtained a copy of George Shoobridge Carr's: "A Synopsis of Elementary Results, a book on Pure Mathematics".

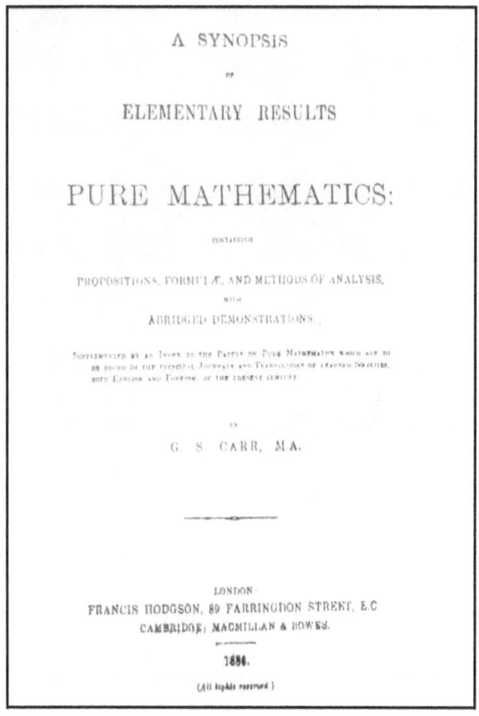

Cover page of the "Synopsis", by George Shoobridge Carr (1837 - 1914).

G.H. Hardy, in his 'Ramanujan: Twelve Lectures suggested by his life and work', says about Carr, a former scholar of Gonville and Caius College, Cambridge: "Carr himself was a private coach in London, who came to Cambridge as an undergraduate when he was nearly forty, and was 12th Senior Optime in the Mathematics Tripos of 1880 (the same year in which he published the first volume of his book).

This book contained propositions, formulae and methods of analysis with abridged proofs published in 1886. It has been reprinted in recent times.

---

46   *ALGEBRA.*

ARITHMETICAL PROGRESSION.

General form of a series in A. P.

79     $a, \; a+d, \; a+2d, \; a+3d, \; \ldots\ldots \; a+(n-1)\,d.$

$a =$ first term,
$d =$ common difference,
$l =$ last of n terms,
$s =$ sum of n terms; then

80     $l = a+(n-1)\,d.$

81     $s = (a+l)\,\dfrac{n}{2}.$

82     $s = \{2a+(n-1)\,d\}\,\dfrac{n}{2}.$

Obtained by writing (79) in reversed order, and adding both series together.

GEOMETRICAL PROGRESSION.

General form of a series in G. P.

83     $a, \; ar, \; ar^2, \; ar^3, \; \ldots\ldots \; ar^{n-1}.$

$a =$ first term,
$r =$ common ratio,
$l =$ last of n terms,
$s =$ sum of n terms; then

84     $l = ar^{n-1}.$

85     $s = a\,\dfrac{r^n-1}{r-1} \quad \text{or} \quad a\,\dfrac{1-r^n}{1-r}.$

If r be less than 1, and n be infinite,

86     $s = \dfrac{a}{1-r}, \quad \text{since} \quad r^n = 0.$

(85) is obtained by multiplying (83) by r, and subtracting one series from the other.

A sample page (p.46) from G.S. Carr's "Synopsis".

This book has become famous due to Ramanujan and has been reprinted by the American Mathematical Society, thanks to the efforts of Bruce C. Berndt, University of Illinois, Champagne-Urbana, USA, in 1999, who wrote about Carr and his 'Synopsis' that:

"He is now completely forgotten, even in his own College, except in so far as Ramanujan has kept his name alive. ... Carr's book covers roughly the subjects of Schedule A of the present Tripos (as these subjects were understood in Cambridge in 1880), and is effectively a 'Synopsis' it professes to be. It contains the enunciations of 6165 theorems, systematically and quite scientifically arranged, with proofs which are often little more than cross-references and are decidedly the least interesting part of the book.

"All this is exaggerated in the famous Notebooks of Ramanujan (which contain no proofs at all), and any student of the Notebooks can see that Ramanujan's ideal of presentation has been copied from Carr's [Synopsis]".

Professor Richard A. Askey (Madison, Wisconsin, USA) has pointed out (in a private communication to the author) the fact that in Carr's Synopsis, formulae in each Chapter are numbered continuously, but the numbering in each Chapter itself starts with 100, 200, etc., discontinuously. Numbers are thus skipped in intermediate places, as well as in certain Chapters, and it is conjectured that this was done perhaps with a view to the possibility of adding new material in approximately the right places in future editions of the book. In all about 1300 numbers are skipped and so, though the last entry bears the number 6165, which Hardy presumed represented the number given by Carr to the last formula as 6165 represented the total number of formulae in the 'Synopsis'.

Note: The importance and influence of the Synopsis on the life and work of Ramanujan has been realized by Ramanujan mathematics specialists, George E. Andrews, Richard A. Askey and Bruce C. Berndt, and their efforts have resulted in this book being reprinted and published in this century.

An actual count of the same was done by Professor Richard A. Askey of the University of Wisconsin, Madison, USA, a renowned specialist in the area of "Special Functions and Orthogonal Polynomials", who has recorded that the actual number of formulas in Carr's 'Synopsis' is actually 4865.

Richard A. Askey, expert in 'Orthogonal Polynomials and Special Functions', renowned for the Askey – Wilson Orthogonal Polynomial scheme. Askey raised funds for a bust of Ramanujan sculpted by Paul Granlund.

An actual count of the same was done by Professor Richard A. Askey of the University of Wisconsin, Madison, USA, a renowned specialist in the area of "Special Functions and Orthogonal Polynomials", who has recorded that the actual number of formulas in Carr's 'Synopsis' is actually 4865.

Carr's 'Synopsis' contains formulae in algebra, analytical geometry, calculus and trigonometry and <u>without proofs.</u> This book is similar to the later day, more recent, compilations like that of, say, "Tables of Integrals, Series, and Products", by I.S. Gradshteyn and I.M. Ryzik, Fifth edition, Academic Press, (New York, 1994). The fact that Ramanujan also noted down results without proofs in his Notebooks has therefore led to the conclusion that the style of recording his Entries in his Notebooks followed by Ramanujan is due to Carr's. There is also the opinion that Carr's 'Synopsis' would not have become renowned to the extent of being reprinted in recent times, at the turn of this century but for Ramanujan.

Professor P.V. Seshu Aiyar and Mr. R. Ramachandra Rao, in their biographical article, in the Collected Papers of Ramanujan, state that: "It was this book which awakened his genius. He set himself to establish the formulae given therein. As he was without the aid of other books, each solution was a piece of research as far as he was concerned".

It is the considered opinion of many that in proving one formula, Ramanujan discovered many others, and thus he laid for himself a foundation for higher mathematics.

During the years 1904 and 1907, Ramanujan started noting the formulae down in his Notebooks. The fact that there were no proofs provided by Carr in his Synopsis turned out to be a boon to Ramanujan who set out on his own mathematical voyage of adventure by proving each one of them for his own pleasure of understanding.

It is the considered opinion of the mathematician E.H. Neville -- who came to teach B.Sc.(Hons.) course at the University of Madras, in 1913 and was commissioned by Hardy with the task of meeting and checking out the credentials of Ramanujan and his Notebooks – that "in proving one formula, he [Ramanujan] discovered many others, and began to compile a note-book" to record his results.

Ramanujan thus laid for himself a concrete foundation for higher mathematics. This was perhaps during the period 1904 to 1910 that he started the habit of noting his formulas in his Notebooks. The first public recognition of the extraordinary mathematical prowess of Ramanujan came when he was awarded the Sri K. Ranganatha Rao special prize at the annual prize distribution ceremony of the Town High School, in 1904, for his proficiency in Mathematics.

S. Narayana Iyer, M.A.,
Treasurer, Madras Port Trust.

Dewan Bahadur R. Ramachandra
Rao, M.A., Collector of Nellore.

University of Madras

CERTIFICATE REQUIRED UNDER SECTION XII. OF THE ACT OF INCORPORATION.

FIRST EXAMINATION IN ARTS.

I hereby certify that Ramanujam S *attended the Junior First Arts Class of the* Kumbakonam *College for three-fourths of the number of working days of the first term of* 1905 *and that his progress and conduct have been satisfactory.*

4 July 1905.

Principal

The Attendance certificate issued to Ramanujan by the University of Madras.

Ramanujan appeared for the "Junior Subrahmanyam Scholarship" examination, in 1904 but for low marks secured in English, he did not get the scholarship. Later encouraged by Professor P.V. Seshu Iyer, he appeared for the examination again and was successful in passing the competitive examination in Mathematics and English composition. This enabled him to secure the Scholarship.

In those days, the University offered a two-year Intermediate course, called the First Examination in Arts, F.A. class during which the students had to study English, Sanskrit, Mathematics, Physiology and History of Rome and Greece.

An anecdote related to his school days is about a class in which a bull-frog was being dissected in a Biology class, which was repulsive to him as he was a strict vegetarian. As a consequence he neglected his study of this subject and Ramanujan is supposed to have returned an answer script with: "Sir, this is the undigested portion of the digestion class".

Needless to say, while this reveals also a sense of humour which he had, it resulted in his failure in the subject. It is said that often he would score a centum in mathematics exams. Unfortunately, he did not pass in English and hence was not promoted to the senior F.A. class in January 1905.

This resulted in the loss of his scholarship. His mother who played a dominant role throughout his life, tried to persuade the Principal of the Government Arts College, to take note of her son's extraordinary mathematical ability and appealed for the continuance of the scholarship, but to no avail. This resulted in a depression, and he left his house without informing any one and it is said that he went on a short visit to Visakhaptnam in search of mathematics tuitions.

A year later, in 1906, he joined the Pachchiyappa's College with the intention of writing the University Examinations again, but fell ill and hence returned to Kumbakonam.

In 1907, he appeared for the F.A. degree examinations as a private candidate but again did not pass. This marked an end to his formal education. It is in 1907, that the 'Analytical Club' was founded by V. Ramaswamy Iyer. Though he never taught in any institution, when he sent a mathematics paper to England for its publication, the reply came to him with 'Professor' prefixed to his name. He was addressed as a Professor from then on by everyone. He founded the Indian Mathematical Society in April 1907 with Pune as its Head Quarters. The Society started its activities under the name Analytic Club and the name was soon changed to Indian Mathematical Club. "After the adoption of a new constitution in 1910, the society acquired its present name, namely, the Indian Mathematical Society. The first president of the Society was B. Hanumantha Rao".

Ramanujan went to his mathematics teachers with a number of original and ingenious results in finite and infinite series. Professor P.V. Seshu Iyer who was his lecturer of mathematics at Government Arts College in Kumbakonam. He was transferred to Presidency College, Madras, which enabled Ramanujan, living in Triplicane to go to meet him when he required some help and encouragement.

Years of Adversity

Hardy has stated in 'Ramanujan: Twelve Lectures ...' that "The Years between 18 and 25 are the critical years in a mathematician's career. ... During the five unfortunate years (1907 – 1912) his genius was misdirected, sidetracked and to a certain extent distorted".

V. Ramswamy Iyer, Founder, Indian Mathematical Society.

Despite the pecuniary circumstances and the stresses and strains of day-to-day existence, Ramanujan started noting down his results in his Notebooks.

Ramanujan crossed the Cauvery River, in a 'parisal' to go to School. Like Cambridge on the banks of the river Cam, the Government Arts College, on the bank of Cauvery, a perennial River, was called the Cambridge of India.

A college-mate of Ramanujan, N. Hari Rao, in his article 'We together in the College', in P.K. Srinivasan's compilation of the 'Letters and Reminiscences', has given an absorbing account and stated that it was Ramanujan who taught him the method of constructing Magic Squares, the subject matter of the first Chapter of his first Notebook, which is 3 pages long and also of the first Chapter of the second Notebook, which is 12 pages long.

Sri P.K. Srinivasan (Nov. 4, 1924 – June 20, 2005) created the Ramanujan Maths Museum and Math Education Center, created in a room in the Avvai Kalai Kazhagam, Royapuram, Chennai. He was a Fulbright Scholar for two years in America. After his return, his untiring efforts during 1962 – 1967 as a mathematics teacher in the Muthialpet High School, in Chennai, resulted in his comprehensive collection of Letters written by Ramanujan or received by Ramanujan and these are today the only and main source for all the material on the life of Srinivasa Ramanujan, along with the series of

Government Arts College, Kumbakonam, on the bank of Cauvery.

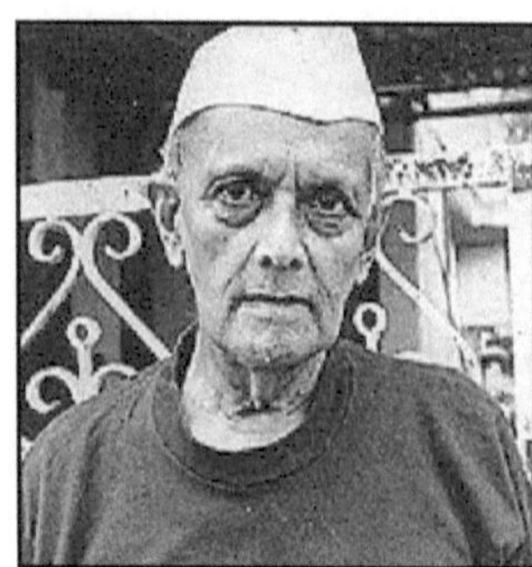

P.K.Srinivasan and a corner view of the exhibits at the Musueum crearted for Ramanujan at the Avvai Kalai Kazhagam, in Royapuram, Chennai.

thityone articles in Tamil, in the magazine section of Dinamani Kadhir, authored by T.V. Rangaswamy, using the pseudonym 'Ragami'. Ragami also brought out the book entitled "Ganithamedhai Ramanujan", published by Pooram Publications, T'Nagar, Chennai – 600017, in Decemebr 1985. Ragami had the advantage of interacting with the wife of Ramanujan, Janakiammal (1899 – 13 April 1994) to gather many facts regarding her marriage and life together before Ramanujan left for England and after his return when she lived with him and nursed him during his terminal illness.

Obviously, the interest in Magic Squares for Ramanujan dates from his School days, and experts opine that this is disconnected with the high level of mathematics in the remainder of the Notebooks, since constructing magic squares is recreational mathematics.

One may conjecture that Ramanujan's expertise in preparing the conflict free time tables for his School inspired him to think of magic squares.

The smallest magic square possible is of 3-dimensions and one magic square for 15 is given below:

4	3	8
9	5	1
2	7	6

A 3 x 3 magic square for 15.

The first biography of Ramanujan, authored by T.V. Rangaswamy (Ragami).
Front and back covers of the book, published by Puram Publications, 1985.

22	12	18	87
70	26	20	23
30	15	78	16
17	86	23	13

22 – 12 – 1887

The 4 x 4 Date Magic Square for 139,
the Date of Birth of Srinivasa Ramanujan.

The row, column, diagonal and skew-diagonal sums all add up to 15 in the case of the 3 x 3 square and to 139 in the case of the 4 x 4 magic square. Note that these are not unique and try to form other 3 x 3 and 4 x 4 magic squares in your spare time.

Magic squares is in the realm of recreational mathematics and though Ramanujan's Notebook 1 and Notebook 2 contain these in the first chapters, the rest of the 16 chapters of Notebook 1 and 21 Chapters of Notebook 2 contain Entries are 3254 each one of them has been considered as a theorem by later day mathematicians who tried hard to provide proofs for each one of them.

A magic square is a square array of usually distinct natural numbers in which the sum of the numbers in each row, column and diagonals (diagonal and skew-diagonal) are equal. In some instances, the requirement of the two diagonal sums is dropped. Ramanujan's investigations in continued fractions and divergent series also started during this period.

Ramanujan's betrothal to nine year old Janaki was in 1908 and the marriage took place at Rajendram, near Karur, in 1909. Robert Kanigel in 'The Man Who KnewInfinity: a life of the Genius Ramanujan' (Scribner's, 1991; Indian edition by Rupa & Co, 1994), constructs a vivid account of this marriage arranged by Komalathammal, not approved by his father (who was not present at the wedding), and dramatizes the foreboding of the impending disaster through the omens preceding the wedding, which was on the brink of being called off due to the late arrival of the bridegroom's party.

Robert Kanigel (photo by Felix Rust) and the cover of his book:
The Man Who Knew Infinity: A lice of the genius Ramanujan'.

During 1906 – 1912, Ramanujan was constantly in search of a benefactor and a job to earn enough for his needs. He tutored a few students in mathematics, in Kumbakonam, and once went in search of tuitions to even Visakhapatnam and sought employment as a tutor in mathematics. Disappointed at the lack of recognition, during this

The Principal J.A. Yades of Pachaiyappa's College, helped Ramanujan by
granting him a Scholarship for his proficiency in mathematics.

trying period, Ramanujan bemoaned to K.S. Viswanatha Sastri – one who became a lawyer and took private tuition in mathematics from Ramanujan – that he was probably destined to die in poverty like Galileo! This was not to be.

In 1910, Ramanujan sought the patronage of Professor V. Ramaswamy Iyer – the Founder of the Indian Mathematical Society – who was then at Tirukkoilur as a Deputy Collector and asked for a Clerical job in his office.

Notebooks of Srinivasa Ramanujan, in the archives of the Library of the University of Madras, in the custody of the Librarian.

The only recommendation Ramanujan had was his valuable Note books which by then contained several results on a gamut of topics, such as: magic squares, prime numbers, infinite series, divergent series, Bernoulli numbers, Riemann zeta function, hypergeometric series, partitions, continued fractions, elliptic functions and modular equations and approximations to p. A scrutiny of the entries in the Notebooks made was sufficient ot convince Ramaswamy Iyer (p. 129 in P.K. Srinivasan's 'Ramanujan: Letters and Reminiscences') that Ramanujan was a gifted mathematician and he [Ramaswamy Iyer] "had no mind to smother his genius by an appointment to the lowest rungs of the revenue department". So, he sent Ramanujan back to Madras with a letter of introduction to Professor P.V. Seshu Iyer, then at the Presidency College, Madras. Professor Seshu Iyer had known Ramanujan as a student at Government Arts College, Kumbakonam, where he himself was employed as a lecturer of mathematics.

They were meeting after a gap of four years and Seshu Iyer was greatly impressed with the contents of the 'well-sized' Notebooks of Ramanujan and so he gave "a note of recommendation to that true lover of mathematics, Dewan Bahadur Ramachandra Rao, who was then the District Collector at Nellore".

The celebrated Notebooks of Ramanujan now in the safe custody of the University of Madras, thanks to Professor G.H. Hardy and the distinguished Library Scientist, Dr. S.R. Ranganathan to whom they were entrusted by Professor Hardy, who told Rangnathan: "he is your countryman and they should be in your country". A facsimile edition of the Notebooks of Ramanujan were first produced by the Tata Institute of Fundamental Research, Bombay, in 1957. These were reprinted twice, on the occasion of the Birth centenary of Ramanujan in 1987 and in 2011, on the occasion of the 125th Birth Anniversary of Ramanujan by the National Board for Higher Mathematics of India.

Kumbakonam–Ramanujan's parental home

Temple Elephant

Chakra – Vadakalai Namam - Sanku Caste Marks in Temples and every orthodox Vaishnavite home

Garuda - Chakra – Thenkalai Namam - Sanku – Hanuman Hanuman Hanuman (Anjaneya)

CHAPTER 3

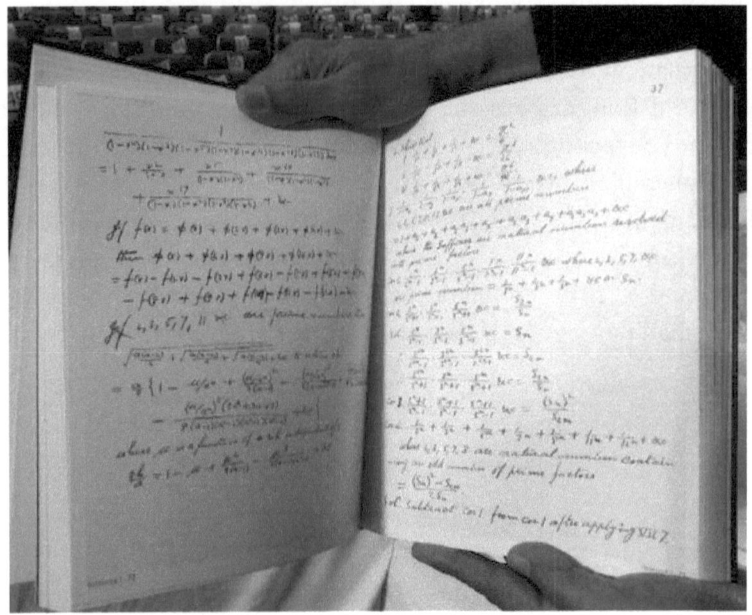

The inside pages (left) of the second edition of Notebooks of Srinivasa Ramanujan, released on the occasion of the 125th birth anniversary celebrations of Ramanujan, in Chennai — The Hindu, Dec. 27, 2011.

A turning point

With the help of his friend, R. Krishna Rao, a nephew of Dewan Bahadur Ramachandra Rao, Ramanujan went to Nellore. On four occasions he could not get an audience and on the fifth occasion, in December 1910, Krishna Rao could meet his uncle with his dear friend Ramanujan. This was a turning point in Ramanujan's life. Years after Ramanujan died, Ramanchandra Rao stated that:

"in the plentitude of my mathematical wisdom, I condescended to permit Ramanujan to walk into my presence" and at that time to Ramachandra Rao, Ramanujan appeared as:

"a short uncouth figure, stout, unshaved, not over-clean, with one conspicuous feature – shining eyes – walked in, with a frayed Notebook under his arm. ... ... He was miserably poor. He had run away from Kumbakonam to get leisure in Madras to pursue his studies. He never craved for any distinction. He wanted leisure, in other words, simple food to be provided for him without exertion, on his part and that he should be allowed to dream on".

Though Ramachandra Rao, an M.A. in mathematics, gave Ramanujan a patient hearing, he took a few days to look into the Notebooks of Ramanujan. At their fourth meeting, when Ramanujan confronted Ramachandra Rao with a letter from Professor Saldanha of Bombay, appreciating the genuineness of his work, Ramachandra Rao started to feel the Ramanujan's work deserved an in depth study by eminent mathematicians. Ramachandra Rao himself states that Ramanujan led him "step-by-step to elliptic integrals and hypergeometric series and at last to his theory of divergent series not yet announced to the world".

Professor P.V. Seshu Aiyer

Professor G. H. Hardy

This converted Ramachandra Rao to become a benefactor and a patron to underwrite Ramanujan's expenses at Madras for some time. He offered to pay him Rs. 20 per month but asked Ramanujan to go to Madras and meet mathematicians there. It is a fact, that Ramanujan never availed of the offer, perhaps because, he could secure an audience to meet him only in his fifth attempt, even though he was accompanied by Ramachandra Rao's nephew!

Professor Seshu Iyer also communicated the earliest contributions of Ramanujan to the Journal of the Indian Mathematical Society, (IMS), in the form of questions, in the 'Questions and Answers to Questions' section of the JIMS. These appeared in 1911 and in his brief illustrious career Ramanujan proposed in all 59 Questions or Answers to Questions in this Journal. One may conjecture, that Ramaswamy Iyer who was seeing a flood of articles from the fertile mathematical mind of Ramanujan, unable to find a suitable journal to publish the same, thought of starting the JIMS, as the solution to the publication problem!

The first 15-page article entitled "Some properties of Bernoulli numbers", of Ramanujan, appeared in the same 1911 volume of the JIMS. In it Ramanujan stated eight theorems embodying arithmetical properties of the Bernoulli numbers*, indicating proofs for three of them; two theorems stated as corollaries of two others, while three theorems are stated as mere conjectures. Professor Seshu Iyer states that "Ramanujan's methods were so terse and novel and his presentation was so lacking in clearness and precision, that the ordinary reader, unaccustomed to such intellectual gymnastics, could hardly follow them".

M.T. Narayanaiengar, an early editor of the JIMS states that the first article of Ramanujan " ... attracted considerable attention. It is however a sad confession to say that the Editor's work in connection with Ramanujan's contribution was by no means light. Ramanujan saw intuitively many things and could not bring himself to explain and the first article had to be referred back to him no less than three times".

The house where S. Narayana Iyer lived in Pycrofts Road.

Ramanujan and Narayna Iyer discussed mathematics using two large slates, in the nights, after Dinner, using slate pencils. This house is still there in Triplicane.

Ramanujan lived in the small house, called 'Summer House', in Sami Pillai Street in Triplicane, Madras, accepting reluctantly a monthly financial assistance from the Collector of Nellore for about a year.

Later he declined this help and from January 12 to February 21, 1912, he worked as a Clerk in the Accountant Gerneral's Office. Not satisfied with this job, Ramanujan apaplied for and secured a post in the Accounts Section, and secured a Class III, Grade IV, Clerical Post, with no specific Responsibilities, thanks to the help of Narayana Iyer, the Manager of Madras Port Trust, who was also the Treasurer of the IMS and a friend of Ramaswamy Iyer and Seshu Iyer. Note: The first few Bernoulli numbers are:

$B_0 = -1$, $B_2 = 1/6$, $B_4 = 1/30$, $B_6 = 1/42$, $B_8 = 1/30$, $B_{10} = 5/66$,

$B_{12} = 691/2730$, ... $B_{38} = 29299939\,13841559/6$, etc.

Obviously, the highly irregular nature of these numbers stimulated Ramanujan.

S. Narayana Iyer was an M.A. in mathematics and a good mathematician who has published research papers. In those days, the British took bright young men into their administrative services, since they wanted a few to help them rule the country.

Narayana Iyer was not only instrumental in Ramanujan being offered a job in the Madras Port Trust, but also in securing the life-long support of Sir Francis Spring to the career of Ramanujan. He was indeed a true friend, philosopher and guide to Ramanujan from the day they met throughout his lifetime.

The role Narayana Iyer played in the life Ramanujan is best recounted in the words of Narayana Iyer's son, N. Subbanarayanan:

S. Thirunarayanan son of Narayana Iyer and Bruce C. Berndt, in recent times, holding the slate used by Ramanujan. Narayana Iyer also used a similar slate.

The slate in the hands of Thirunarayanan, son of S. Narayana Iyer, is now preserved by his descendents as a family heirloom.

"To illustrate the depth of his genius, I can quote on of the incidents which happened during the stay of Sri Ramanujan with my father when we were living in No. 580, Pycrofts Road, Triplicane. During that period, every night both Ramanujan and my father used to work Mathematics in two big sized slates sitting on a small parapet upstairs. This used to be carried on till about 11.30 p.m. and was a source of nuisance to other inmates of the housed who used to sleep in the adjoining rooms. I distinctly remember the noises of the slate pencils which used to be a background music for my sleep. Several nights I have seen Ramanujan get up at 2 o'clock in the night and note down something in the slate in the dull light of a hurricane lamp. When my father asked him what he was writing, he used to say that he worked out mathematics in his dreams and now he was jotting the results in the slate to remember them.

"Evidently, this goes to show that he must have had a remarkable power of subconscious working and grasp of intellectual strides in mathematics. Peculiarly enough, my father used to ask Ramanujan some doubts in these jottings. Between one step and another step there used to be a big gap. My father, being a fairly good mathematician himself, was unable to capture the strides of Ramanujan's discoveries. He used to tell him, "When I am not able to understand your steps, I do not know how other mathematicians of a critical nature will accept your genius. You must descend to my level and write at least ten steps between the two steps of yours".

Sri Ramanujan used to say, 'When it is so simple and clear to me, why should I write more steps?' But somehow my father slowly got him round, cajoled him and made him write some more, though it used to be a mighty task of boredom to him".

Mr. Narayana Iyer requested for and obtained the slate used by Ramanujan as a memento, in exchange of his slate and it is still a heir-loom with the family of late Mr. Subbanarayanan. It is interesting to note that Mr. Narayana Iyer used too send his son Subbanarayanan to borrow a book on Elliptic Functions from the Library of the University of Madras.

Dewan Bahadur Ramachandra Rao also wrote to Sir Francis Spring, Chairman of the Madras Port Trust, about Ramanujan.

Ramanujan's entry into the Madras Port Trust, on March 1, 1912, may well be considered as the most significant turning point in Ramanujan's career.

He held this clerical post at Port Trust for a period of 14 months. His wife Janaki joined him during this period and Ramanujan shifted his residence to Saiva Muthiah Mudali Street in George Town, then the heart of Madras city. This period marks the beginning of the appreciation of Ramanujan's scholarship and researches in mathematics.

Left: earliest photo of Janaki, as a seamstress eking out a livelihood.
Second: the Port Trust celebrated the 75th Birth Anniversary of Ramanujan.

Dewan Bahadur Ramachandra Rao induced Professor C.L.T. Griffith, of the Engineering College, Madras, to take interest in Ramanujan and Griffith wrote in November 1912 to Sir Francis Spring, the Chairman of Madras Port Trust about the 'very poor accountant' who was 'a most remarkable mathematician' and asking him to keep Ramanujan "happily employed until something can be done to make use of his extraordinary gifts".

Professor Griffith also wrote to Professor M.J.M. Hill of the University College, University of London, on Ramanujan's work and he received a reply in December 1912. Unfortunately, Professor Hill could not find time to study the results. He observed that "the book which will be most useful to him is Bromwich's Theory of Infinite Series, published by Cambridge University Press (or Macmillan)" and gave advice as to how Ramanujan could get his papers published. In a sequel to this reply, dated 7 December 1912, Professor Hill wrote to Professor Griffith:

"Mr. Ramanujan is evidently a man with a taste of Mathematics, and with some ability, but he has got on the wrong lines. He does not understand the precautions which have to be taken in dealing with divergent series, oterwise he could not have obtained the erroneous results you send me, viz:-

$$1 + 2 + 3 + \ldots + \infty = - 1/12,$$

$$1^2 + 2^2 + 3^2 + \ldots + \infty^2 = 0,$$

$$1^3 + 2^3 + 3^3 + \ldots + \infty^3 = 1/240.$$

The sums of n terms of these infinite series are, respectively:

$$n(n+1)/2, \quad n(n+1)(2n+1)/6, \quad [n(n+1)/2]^2$$

and they all tend to ∞ as n tends to ∞. I do think you can do no better for him than to get him a copy of the book I recommended, Bromwhich's Theory of Infinite Series, published by Macmillan and Co., who have branches in Calcutta and Bombay. Price Rs.15/- net."

Ramanujan published two short notes, one

"On question 330 of Professor Sanjana"

and another a

"Note on a set of simultaneous equations",

in the JIMS, in 1912. When Ramanujan approached Professor Seshu Iyer with some theorems on Prime Numbers, his attention was drawn to G.H. Hardy's Tract on 'Orders of Infinity'. Ramanujan observed that "on p. 36 of this Tract the exact order of r(x) has not yet been determined", where r(x) is defined by the equation:

$$\rho(x) = \pi(x) - \int_{2}^{x} dt / (\log t)$$

where $\pi(x)$ denotes the number of primes less than x. In other words, "no definite expression has yet been found for the number of primes less than any given number".

Ramanujan told Professor Seshu Iyer that he had discovered a result which gave the order of $\rho(x)$. This prompted Professor Seshu Iyer to suggest the communication of this and other results to Mr. G.H. Hardy – a Fellow of the Royal Society and Cayley Lecturer in Mathematics at the Cambridge University – by then a world famous mathematician who was ten years Ramanujan's senior.

The first (11-pages) long letter of Ramanujan to Hardy, dated January 16, 1913, has become a historic letter. While more about the contents of this letter and its impact will follow, here we draw attention to only what Ramanujan said on divergent series, in that letter to Hardy:

"I have got theorems on divergent series, theorems to calculate the convergent values corresponding to the divergent series, viz.:

$$1 - 2 + 3 - 4 + \ldots = 1/4,$$
$$1 - 1! + 2! - 3! + \ldots = 0.596,$$
$$1 + 2 + 3 + 4 + \ldots = -1/12,$$
$$1^3 + 2^3 + 3^3 + 4^3 + \ldots = 1/240.$$

Two books authored by G.H. Hardy which are considered as classics.

"As instances of these 3 classes I may mention … … Ramanujan's second (10-pages) letter dated February 27, 1913, was in response to Hardy's reply. In this letter Ramanujan wrote:

"I find in many a place in your letter rigourous proofs are required and so on and you ask me to communicate the methods of proof. I am sure you will follow the London Professor. But as a fact I did not give him any proof but made some assertions as the following under my new theory. I told him that the sum of an infinite number of terms of the series:

$$1+2+3+4+ \times\times\times + \infty = - 1/12$$

under my theory.

"If I tell you this you will at once point out to me the lunatic asylum as my goal. I dilate on this simply to convince you that you will not be able to follow my method of proofs if I indicate the lines on which I proceed in a single letter. You may ask how you can accept results based on wrong premises.

"What I tell you is this. Verify the results I give and if they agree with your results, got by treading on the groove in which the present day mathematicians move, you should at least grant me that there may be some truth in my fundamental basis. So what I now want at this stage is for eminent professors like you to recognize that there some worth in me. I am already a half starving man. To preserve my brains I want food and this is now my first consideration.

"Any sympathetic letter from you will be helpful to me here to get a scholarship either from the University or from the Government.

… … … … … … … … … … … … … … … … … …… … … … … …

"You may judge me hard that I am silent on the methods of proof. I have to reiterate that I may be misunderstood if I give in a short compass the lines on which I proceed. It is not on account of my unwillingness on my part but because I fear I shall not be able ot explain everything in a letter. I do not mean that the methods should be buried with me. I shall have them published if my results are recognized by eminent men like you".

The passages quoted clearly indicate that Ramanujan was fully aware of the apparently absurd nature of the results and also the difficulty he had in an unambiguous presentation of his 'startling' results. In the words of Bruce C. Berndt and Robert A. Rankin, in 'Ramanujan: Letters and Commenary' (p. 17):

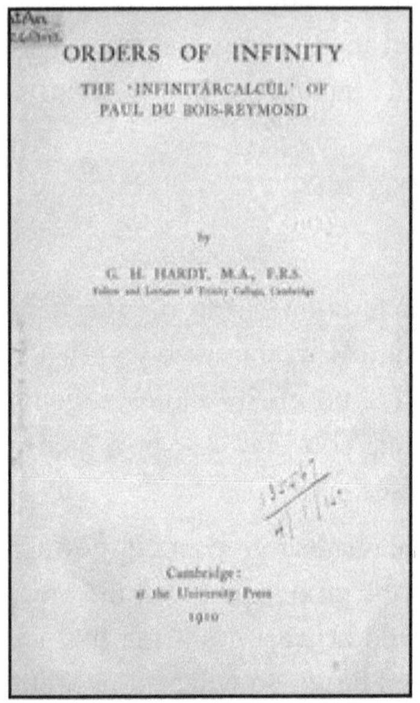

Orders of Infinity

Professor G.H. Hardy, M.A., F.R.S.

"Evidently, Hill shared Abel's view that 'divergent series are in general deadly', for, not surprisingly, he failed to discern the origin of the three results quoted in his letter. The three claims give the values of $z(-n)$, for $n = 1, 2, 3$, respectively. It was natural for Ramanujan to write these facts in terms of the divergent series of the Riemann zeta-function to these values. In Ramanujan's theory of the 'constant' of a (convergent or divergent) series, the three values of $-1/12$, 0 and $1/240$ are, respectively, the constants of the three given series.

"It is likely that this theory was not communicated to Hill. Ramanujan's theory of divergent series is elucidated, albeit rather imprecisely, in Chapter 6 of his second Notebook and readers should consult Berndt's book for an account of this theory".

The Years of fruition

The life of Ramanujan in the words of C.P. Snow "is an admirable story and one which showers credit on nearly everyone" – this quotation is from the Foreword to G.H. Hardy's 'A Mathematician's Apology' (Cambridge University Press, 1976, p.30), wherein he wrote: "Hardy was not the first eminent mathematician to be sent the Ramanujan manuscripts. There had been two before him, both English, both of the highest professional standard. They had each returned the manuscripts without comment.

I don't think history related what they said, if anything, when Ramanujan became famous." As for their identity, Snow adds that:

"out of chivalry Hardy concealed this in all that he said or wrote about Ramanujan. A. Nandy in his book, "Alternative Sciences" (Allied Publishers, New Delhi, 1980), claims that the two are H.F. Baker and E.W. Hobson. Though they did not respond to the letter from Ramanujan in India, after Ramanujan was recognized by Hardy and they came into contact with him in Cambridge, they were willing to support the candidature of Ramanujan for a Fellowship of the Royal Society, London, in the category of "those with personal knowledge".

Henry Frederick Baker
(1866 – 1956)

Ernest William Hobson
(1856 – 1933)

From then on, Sir Francis Spring, the Chairman of Madras Port Trust and S. Narayana Iyer, the Manager of Port Trust, gave Ramanujan every possible encouragement. Dr. Gilbert T. Walker, F.R.S., who was the Director General of Observatories in Simla, visited the University of Madras, in February 1913, and Sir Francis Spring drew his attention to the Notebooks of Ramanujan.

Dr. G.T. Walker, a mathematician, was a Senior Wrangler and a former Fellow of Trinity College, Cambridge, and a Lecturer. He immediately recognized the intrinsic quality of the work of Ramanujan. He wrote to Mr. Francis Dewsbury, the Registrar of the University of Madras, commending the work of Ramanujan to be "comparable in originality with that of a Mathematics Fellow in a Cambridge College", though lacking in precision and completeness necessary for establishing the universal validity of the results.

Mr. Dewsbury wrote that it was perfectly clear to him "that the University would be justified in enabling S. Ramanujan for a few years at least to spend the whole of his time on mathematics without any anxiety as to his livelihood". He also wanted the University to correspond with Hardy, Fellow of Trinity College, Cambridge, since Ramanujan was already in correspondence with Hardy, assuring Hardy of the interest of the University in Ramanujan.

We reproduce here the letter written by Ramanujan, to the Chief Accountant of the Madras Port Trust, on February 9, 1912, below. (It is possible that this letter was drafted for Ramanujan by Mr. S. Narayana Iyer, who was at that time the Treasurer of the Madras Port Trust.

The recommendation of Dr. Walker was accepted by the Board of Studies of the University of Madras and Ramanujan was granted a special Research Scholarship of Rs. 75/- per month for two years with express consent of Lord Pentland, the Governor of Madras, with the condition that Ramanujan should submit Quarterly Reports on his work.

It should be noted that Ramanujan was at that time getting a salary of Rs. 25/- per month, for one month, in the office of the

Accountant General (A.G.'s Office), with no responsibilities, and Rs. 30/- per month, for a year, when he was a Grade III, Class IV, Clerk at the Madras Port Trust. (The salary of a Professor in those days was Rs. 225/- per month.) To enable Ramanujan to accept this offer of the <u>first ever Research Scholarship</u>, in any subject, by the University of Madras, the Port Trust authorities granted him two years leave on loss of pay. Thus began the illustrious research career of Ramanujan as a professional mathematician.

As pointed out, this first letter of Ramanujan to Hardy, dated January 16, 1913, is today considered a historic letter. It read:

Dr. G.T. Walker,F.R.S.,
Director General (1904-1924),
Indian Meteorological
Society, Simla.

Sir Francis Spring, Chairman,
Madras Port Trust.

"Dear Sir,

"I beg to introduce myself to you as a clerk in the Accounts Department of the Port Trust Office at Madras on a salary of only pounds 20 per annum. I am now about 23 years of age. I have had no University education but I have undergone the ordinary school course. After leaving school I have been employing the spare time at my disposal to work at Mathematics. I have not trodden through the conventional regular course which is followed in a University course, but I am striking out a new path for myself. I have made a special investigation of divergent series in general and the results I get are termed by local mathematicians as 'startling' …

"I would request you to go through the enclosed papers. Being poor, if you are convinced that there is anything of value I would like to have my theorems published. I have not given the actual investigations nor the expressions that I get but I have indicated the lines on which I proceed. Being inexperienced I would very highly value any advice you give me. Requesting you to be excused for the trouble I give you,

"I remain, Dear Sir, Yours truly,

(sd.) SRamanujan."

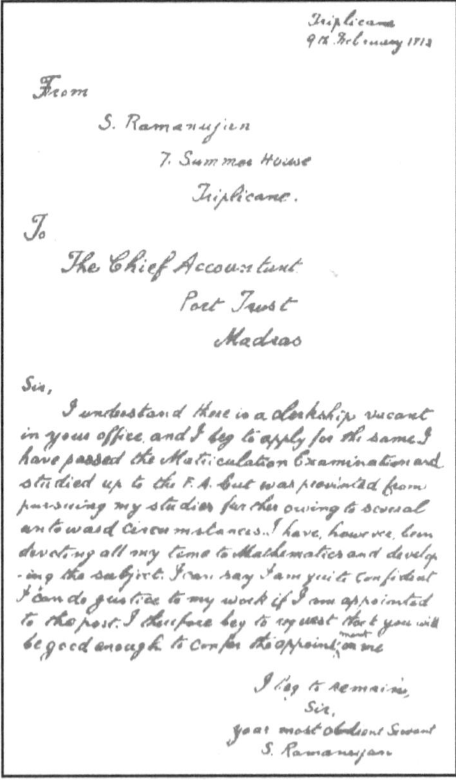

A letter written by Ramanujan seeking a job at the Madras Port Trust.

Hardy's prompt reply dated February 8, 1913, was the starting point of Ramanujan's recognition by the Western world of mathematicians and this most encouraging response read:

"Dear Sir,

"I was exceedingly interested by your letter and by the theorems which you state. You will however understand that, before I can judge properly of the value of what you have done, it is essential that I should see proofs of some of your assertions.

"Your results seem to me to fall into roughly 3 classes:

1. there are a number of results which are already known, or are easily deducible from known theorems;
2. there are results which, so far as I know, are new and interesting, but interesting rather from their curiosity and apparent difficulty thatn their importance;
3. (3) there are results which appear to be new and important, but in which almost everything depends on the precise rigour of the methods of proof which you have used."

Hardy continued in this historic letter examples of the three classes of results he discerned. Ramanujan in his second (10 pages long) letter dated February 27, 1913, was in response to Hardy's reply. In it he wrote:

"I find in many a place in your letter rigorous proofs are required and so on and you ask me to communicate the methods of proof. I am sure you will follow the London Professor.

"But as a fact I did not give him any proof but made some assertions as the following under my new theory. I told him that the sum of an infinite number of terms of the series: $1+2+3+4+ \ldots = -1/12$ under my theory. If I tell you this you will at once point out to me the lunatic asylum as my goal. I dilate on this simply to convince that that you will not be able to follow my method of proofs if I indicate the lines on which I proceed in a single letter. You may ask how you can accept results based on wrong premises. What I tell you is this. Verify the results I give and if they agree with your results, got by treading the on the groove in which the present day mathematicians move, you should at least grant me that there may be some truth in my fundamental basis. So what I now want at this stage is for eminent professors like you to recognize that there is some worth in me. I am already a half starving man. To preserve my brains I want food and this is now my first consideration. Any sympathetic letter from you will be helpful to me here to get a scholarship either from the University or from the Government.

… … … … … … … … … … … … … … … … … …… … … … … …

"You may judge me hard that I am silent on the methods of proof. I have to reiterate that I may be misunderstood if I give in a short compass the lines on which I proceed. It is not an account of my unwillingness on my part but because I fear I shall not be able to explain everything in a letter. I do not mean that the methods should be buried with me. I shall have them published if my results are recognized by eminent men like you."

The passages quoted from the letter indicate that Ramanujan was fully aware of the apparently absurd nature of the results and also the difficulty he had in an unambiguous presentation of his 'startling' results. In the words of Bruce C. Berndt and Robert A. Rankin, p.17, in their "Ramanujan: Letters and Reminiscences": "Evidently, Hill shared Abel's view that 'divergent series are in general deadly', for, not surprisingly, he failed to discern the origin of the three results quoted in his letter. The three claims give the values of z(-n), for n=1,2,3, respectively. It was natural for Ramanujan to write these facts in terms of the divergent series of the Riemann zeta-function to these values.

In Ramanujan's theory of the 'constant' of a (convergent or divergent) series, the three values -1/12, 0 and 1/240 are, respectively, the constants of the three given series.

It is likely that this theory was not communicated to Hill. Ramanujan's theory of divergent series is elucidated, albeit rather imprecisely, in Chapter 6 of his second Notebook and readers should consult Berndt's book (Ramanujan's Notebooks, Part - II) for an account of this theory".

The life of Ramanujan in the words of C.P. Snow – in his Foreword to "A Mathematician's Apology", by G.H. Hardy (Cambridge University Press, 1967) – "is an admirable story, and one which showers credit on nearly everyone. Sir Francis Spring, the Chairman and S. Narayana Iyer, the Manager of Port Trust gave Ramanujan every possible encouragement. Dr. Gilbert T. Walker, F.R.S., Director General of Observatories, Simla, visited the University of Madras in February 1913, and Sir Francis Spring did not miss the opportunity to draw his attention to the Notebooks of Ramanujan.

Srinivasa Ramanujan (middle) with fellow scientists at Cambridge

CHAPTER 4

Dr. Walker, a good mathematician and a Senior Wrangler, was a former Fellow of Trinity College, as well as a lecturer in the Cambridge University. He recognized the intrinsic quality of the work of Ramanujan and he had no hesitation in writing to Francis Dewsbury, the Registrar of the University of Madras, commending the work of Ramanujan to be "comparable in originality with that of a Mathematics Fellow in a Cambridge college", though lacking in the precision and completeness necessary for establishing the universal validity of the results. Dewsbury wrote that it was perfectly clear to him "that the University would be justified in enabling S. Ramanujan for a few years at least to spend the whole of his time on mathematics without any anxiety as to his livelihood". The Registrar, Dewsbury also wanted the University to correspond with Mr. Hardy, Fellow of Trinity College, Cambridge, since Ramanujan was already in correspondence with him, assuring Mr. Hardy of the interest of the University in Ramanujan. The recommendation of Dr. Walker was accepted by the Board of Studies of the University of Madras.

The Presidency College, Madras.

Senate House, University of Madras.

Ramanujan was granted a special first ever research scholarship of the University of Rs. 75/- per month for two years with the express consent of Lord Pentland, the Governor of Madras Presidency, with the condition that Ramanujan should submit Quarterly Reports on his work to the University.

The Madras Port Trust immediately granted Ramanujan two years leave, on loss of pay, to enable him to accept the Scholarship from May 1913. Thus began the research career of Ramanujan as a professional mathematician and from the realm of the unknown to world acclaim as a mathematical Genius and from rags to riches.

Leonhard EULER *Carl Friedrich GAUSS* *Srinivasa RAMANUJAN*
(15 Apr.1707–18 *(30 Apr.1777–23* *(22 Dec. 1887–26*
Sep.1783) *Feb.1855)* *Apr.1920)*

Ramanujan's first letter to G.H. Hardy, dated January 16, 1913, contained "the bare statements of about 120 theorems, mostly formal identities from the Notebooks" of his. This collection obviously represented what Ramanujan himself considered as significant results in mathematics obtained by him. The professional mathematician Hardy was aware that he was "the first really competent person who had the chance to see some of his work", found some of the series formulae intriguing, some of the integral formulae which were classical were known and vaguely familiar to him, and some of the integral formulae he could prove with effort but these were to him the least impressive. However, he found that some of Ramanujan's formulae were "on a different level and obviously both difficult and deep".

The renowned writer, C.P. Snow, in his Rectorial Address delivered before the University of St. Andrews, Scotland, on April 13, 1962, vividly records Hardy's reactions to this letter of Ramanujan: "Hardy gave the manuscript a perfunctory glance, and went on reading the morning paper. It occurred to Hardy that the first page was a little out of the ordinary for a cranky correspondent. It seemed to consist of some theorems, very strange-looking theorems, without any argument. Hardy then decided that the man must be a fraud, and duly went about the day according to his habits, giving a lecture, playing a game of tennis. But, there was something nagging at the back of his mind. Anyone who could fake such theorems right or wrong must be a fraud of genius.

Was it more or less likely that there should be a fraud of genius or an unknown Indian mathematician of genius? He went that evening after dinner to argue it out with his collaborator, J.E. Littlewood, whom Hardy always insisted was a better mathematician than himself. They soon had no doubt about the answer. Hardy was seeing the work of someone whom, for natural genius, he could not touch, – who, in natural genius, though of course not in achievement, as Hardy said later, belong to the class of Euler and Gauss".

Hardy made up his mind that Ramanujan should be brought to Cambridge and provided with the necessary education and contact with Western Mathematicians of the highest class. So, Hardy wrote to the Secretary of the Indian Students association, in the Inda Office, London, suggesting that some means be found to get Ramanujan to Cambridge. Hardy in turn wrote, in February 1913, to Mr. Arthur Davies, the Secretary to the Advisory Committee for Indian Students in Madras conveying the desire of the Tutors of Trinity College, to get Ramanujan to Camridge. Thus, began the incredibly true story of Ramanujan's transition from Kumbakonam on the banks of the river Cauvery to Cambridge on the banks of the river Cam.

Ramanujan had to cross the river to go his School in Kumbakonam from his house in a boat called a 'parisal' in Tamil.

In quick succession, Ramanujan received in the next three months four long letters from Hardy in which the latter wrote plainly about what had been proved or claimed to have been proved by Ramanujan. He clearly communicated his genuine anxiety to "see what can be done to give" Ramanujan "a better chance of making the best use of your obvious mathematical gifts". At last Ramanujan found a sympathetic friend in Hardy and was willing to place unreservedly in his hands all that he had.

Quadrangle in the Trinity College. River Cam ran through Cambridge. There were several bridges across Cam.

In quick succession, Ramanujan received in the next three months four long letters from Hardy in which the latter wrote plainly about what had been proved or claimed to have been proved by Ramanujan. He clearly communicated his genuine anxiety to "see what can be done to give" Ramanujan "a better chance of making the best use of your obvious mathematical gifts". At last Ramanujan found a sympathetic friend in Hardy and was willing to place unreservedly in his hands all that he had.

He wrote again to Hardy on February 27, 1913, and sent him more formulae and explanations. On April 17, 1913, Ramanujan wrote to Hardy about his having secured the scholarship of £60 per annum, of the University of Madras, for two years. Ramanujan took up residence at Hanumantharayan Koil Lane in Triplicane around this time and had, access to the books on Mathematics in the Library of Madras University. Being an orthodox Brahmin, from an Iyengar family, Ramanujan was initially reluctant to go abroad because of his own caste prejudices, which were compounded by the extremely orthodox views of his mother to whom he was greatly attached.. Crossing the oceans was considered a sacrilege by the Brahmins and one who did so, on his return to India, was treated as an outcaste and all relationships with the individual and even his family were severed!

At the beginning of 1914, Mr. E.H. Neville, a young mathematician and a Fellow of Trinity College, Cambridge, came as a visiting lecturer to give a course of Lectures on Differential Geometry to the Mathematics Honours students of the University of Madras. Hardy entrusted Neville with the mission of persuading Ramanujan to visit Cambridge.

Once Neville came into contact with Ramanujan and saw the Notebooks of Ramanujan he was convinced of the uncommon ability of Ramanujan and Neville started taking all the required steps for an Indian to go to England. In the process, he overcame all the hurdles in arranging for a smooth passage of Ramanujan to join Trinity College, Cambridge.

E.H. Neville

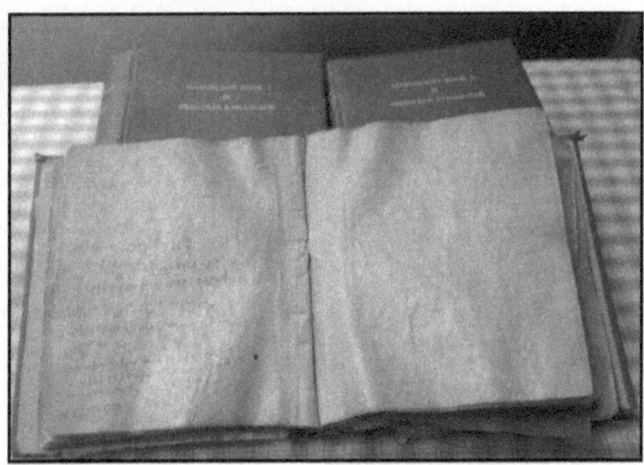

The Notebooks of Ramanujan (Madras Univ.)

Professor Littlehailes, who was a Professor of Mathematics with the observatory in Madras introduced Neville "to everyone who carried weight in the University or in the civil administration; everywhere I talked of Ramanujan, explained as I have tried to do now the importance to him of a stay in Cambridge, and urged generosity".

In a letter, dated January 18, 1914, to Mr. Dewsbury, the Registrar of the University of Madras, Neville wrote about "the importance of securing to Ramanujan a training in the refinements of modern methods and a contact with men who know what range of ideas have been explored and what have not" and prophesied that Ramanujan would respond to such a Professor Littlehailes, who was a Professor of Mathematics with the observatory in Madras introduced Neville "to everyone who carried weight in the University or in the civil administration; everywhere I talked of Ramanujan, explained as I have tried to do now the importance to him of a stay in Cambridge, and urged generosity".

In a letter, dated January 18, 1914, to Mr. Dewsbury, the Registrar of the University of Madras, Neville wrote about "the importance of securing to Ramanujan a training in the refinements of modern methods and a contact with men who know what range of ideas have been explored and what have not" and prophesied that Ramanujan would respond to such a stimulus that "his name will become one of the greatest in the history of mathematics, and the University and city of Madras will be proud to have assisted in his passage from obscurity to fame".

The very next day, Professor Littlehailes also wrote to Mr. Dewsbury that Ramanujan "be granted by this University a scholarship of about £ 250 (Sterling) together with a grant of about £ 100 in order to enable him to proceed to Cambridge. Ramanujan is a man of most remarkable mathematical ability, amounting I might say to genius, whose light is metaphorically hidden under a bushel in Madras".

They wrote these letters after Ramanujan was persuaded to put aside his prejudices against crossing the sea. Hardy stated that Ramanujan's "consent was at lost got very easily ... [when] his mother announced that she had a dream in which she saw her son seated in a big hall amidst a group of Europeans and that the goddess of Namagiri had commanded her son fulfilling his life's purpose".

The proposals regarding the grant of the scholarship to Ramanujan were approved by the University of Madras. To the lasting credit of the University, the Syndicate decided within a week to set aside Rs.10,000/- to offer Ramanujan a scholarship of £ 250 a year plus £ 100 for a passage by ship and for initial outfit. The second class fare between Bombay and London was £ 32 in 1914, or about Rs. 480. At the instance of Professor Neville, and Professor Littlehailes, Sir Francis Spring, the Chairman of Madras Port Trust, wrote to Mr. C.B. Cotterell, the personal secretary to Lord Pentland, the Governor of Madras, persuading his Excellency to speedily approve the University's sanction. The sanction too was granted within a week.

To overcome the caste prejudices, Ramanujan accompanied by Narayana Iyer went to Namakkal and there in a four pillared 'mandapam' botheof them slept on three consecutive nights, with the permission of the temple authorities who locked the temple in the nights as is customary. On the second night, Ramanujan suddenly woke up and excitedly told his friend, philosopher and guide, Narayana Iyer, that he had a dream and in it, the goddess Namagiri told him that he should go to England.

Simultaneously, the mother Komalathammal also had a dream in which she saw her son 'chinnasami' sitting in the company of foreigners at a table and was discussing mathematics with them.

The offer of the University of Madras came to Ramanujan in February 1914. Ramanujan sent his wife Janaki and mother Komalathammal back to Kumbakonam, changed his traditional hairstyle of the Brahmin, viz. a tuft, and got his hair trimmed in to the western style crop before he left Madras harbour, by s.s. Nevasa on March 17, 1914. Prior to his departure, he arranged with the University for £ 60 a year to be sent to his parents in Kumabkonam, out of his annual scholarship amount.

These dreams were considered as revelations of the Goddess granting permission for Ramanujan to go overseas ignoring the caste prejudices of friends and relatives.

It is remarkable that while there was no one in the Colleges or the University who could appreciate the depth of Ramanujan's mathematical abilities, the University of Madras awarded its first ever research scholarship to Ramanujan to enable him to go to Cambridge, despite the fact that he was a failed F.A. of the University of Madras. This is undoubtedly due to the courage of conviction of the Indian stalwarts of that era – Dewan Bahadur Ramachandra Rao, V. Ramaswamy Iyer, S. Narayana Iyer and P.V. Seshu Iyer – who succeeded in convincing and persuading the British authorities to act immediately on the basis of the merits of the candidate.

Namakkal Temple

Goddess Namagiri of Namakkal, an inner 'gopuram' and God Narasimha.
(Left: The 'Moolavar' is in granite; 'uthsavar' in 'panchaloha' is in the front.)

The rapidity with which the Chairman of Port Trust, Sir Francis Spring, obtained the backing of the academic bodies, and the approval of the Chancellor of the University, Lord Pentland, through the Registrar, Mr. Dewsbury, is remarkable, extraordinary and unusual.

It is indeed surprising that there is no mention anywhere of the name of the Vice Chancellor of the University of Madras at the time of Ramanujan's rise to fame. Sir John Wallis was the Vice Chancellor during the period 1908 – 1916. Dr. V. Thangaraj, Director of the Ramanujan Institute for Advanced Study in Mathematics, obtained this information from the University's Administrative office in Chepauk:

A minor point of interest, for the historian, is to try to understand why in all the available correspondence there is no mention of the Vice Chancellor's name and everything required in the form of financial support and sanctions of the University, was obtained by Mr. Dewsbury, the Registrar, without any semblance of bureaucratic interference, to support the exceptional genius that was Ramanujan.

Mr. Arthur Davies, and Professor Littlehailes attended to all the relevantdetails regarding Ramanujan's passage to England. Except for the first three days when he was sea-sick, Ramanujan enjoyed the voyage and reached London through the Channel and the river Thames on April 14, 1914 (the Tamil New Year's day). Ramanujan was received by Neville and his brother at the Docks and he stayed at Cornwell Road for a few days before going to Cambridge on the evening of April 18. He remained for a few days in Neville's house before moving to the college premises for his stay, which even though costlier than lodging houses, was more convenient for him and the professors.

Ramanujan wrote to his friend, R. Krishan Rao, that:

"Mr. Hardy, Mr. Neville and others here are unassuming, kind and obliging. As soon as I came here, Mr. Hardy paid £20 to the college for my entrance and other fees and made arrangements to give me a scholarship of £40 a year".

Ramanujan was admitted by Mr. Hardy to Trinity College which supplemented his scholarship with the award of an 'exhibition' of £60 a year, to augment the £250 a year scholarship awarded by the University of Madras, possibly because Ramanujan had already requested the University to set aside and send £60 to his parents in Madras.

Though Ramanujan had access only to Carr's Synopsis – and perhaps, to few other books available at the Library of the University of Madras – still in the words of the historian J.R. Newman, in his book entitled "Srinivasa Ramanujan", in 'Mathematics in the modern World' (W.H. Freeman & Co., (1968) pages 73 – 76, Ramanujan "arrived in England abreast and often head of contemporary mathematical knowledge. Thus, in a lone mighty sweep, he had succeeded in recreating in his field, through his own un-aided powers, a rich half century of European mathematics. One may doubt whether so prodigious a feat had ever before been accomplished in the history of thought".

To Hardy, Ramanujan's friend, philosopher and discoverer "The limitation of his knowledge was as startling as its profundity. Here was a man who could work out modular equations, and theorems of complex multiplications, to orders unheard of, whose mastery of continued fractions was, on he formal side at any rate, beyond that of any mathematician in the world, who had found for himself the functional equation of the zeta-function, and the dominant terms of many of the most famous problems in the analytic theory of numbers, and he had never heard of a doubly periodic function or of Cauchy's theorem, and had indeed but the vaguest idea of what a functions of a complex variable was.

His ideas of what constituted a mathematical proof were of the most shadowy description. All his results, new or old, right or wrong, had been arrived at by a process of mingled argument, intuition and induction, of which he was entirely unable to give a coherent account".

With such a natural genius, Hardy collaborated and tried to teach, as he wrote, as quoted in Kanigel's 'Man who Knew Infinity', that the "things of which it was impossible that he should remain in ignorance. ... It was impossible to allow him to go through life supposing that all the zeroes of the zeta function were real. So, I had to try to teach him, and in a measure I succeeded, though I obviously learnt from him much more than he learnt from me."

Hardy and Littlewood at Trinity College.

Hardy – Littleweed collaboration is unique.

Hardy did not attempt to convert Ramanujan into a mathematician of the modern school but enabled him to go on producing original ideas in his classical mould with rigourous proofs for the theorems he discovered.

The period of Ramanujan's stay in England almost overlapped with the years in which World War I took place. "One of the lecturers went to war" wrote Ramanujan to his friend Krishna Rao, in Madras, and he felt that "the other professors … lost interest owing to the … war".

One of the professors remarked that Ramanujan was in England at the most unfortunate time. There were about 700 students before the war, but this number reduced to 150 by November 1915. Fortunately, Hardy did not get drafted for the war while his senior Littlewood could not escape the drafting.

Ramanujan initially asked for and obtained some South Indian food items like tamarind, coconut oil, and such other essential ingredients for cooking his vegetarian South Indian meal. These were sent to him by his family members, by post parcel from his home in Madras, as well as from a company in London. But by January 1915, he wrote to his friend S.M. Subramanian in India that:

"now as well as in the future I am not in need of anything as I gained control over my taste and can live on mere rice with a little salt and lemon juice for an indefinite time".

His "difficulty of getting proper food" was alleviated by the availability of good milk and fruits. Ramanujan being a strict vegetarian, had no option but to cook for himself. When in the 1980s investigations were on as to what exactly was the cause of his death, there was a query to me by Bruce Berndt asking me whether the cause of Ramanujan's untimely death was due to lead poisoning !

It is possible Ramanujan might have carried with him an 'ever silver' vessel and cooked his lintel-tamarind-soup in it. This is the explanation which I could come up with to explain the chance of Ramanujan's death being due to lead poisoning! (Note: Often these days, by the 1980s, one can buy the 'sambar' powder and 'rasam' powder in special oriental shops and even in larger supermarkets in England, which have sizeable Indian communities.)

One day Ramanujan was attending a lecture by Mr. Berry at the University on Elliptic Integrals. Mr. Berry was working out some formulae on the balck board and when he glanced at Ramanujan found his face flushed with excitement. So Mr. Berry asked whether

Ramanujan was following his lecture and whether he had anything to say. At this opportunity Ramanujan went to the black board and much to everyone's amazement wrote down some of the results which were yet to be proved by Mr. Berry.

P.C. Mahalanobis

This anecdote has been recalled by a contemporary of Ramanujan, Professor P.C. Mahalanobis, (and found in Part I of P.K. Srinivasan's "Ramanujan: Letters and Reminiscences"), the eminent Indian Statistician and the founder Director of the Indian Statistical Institute in Calcutta.

The Indian Statistical Institute, Calcutta.

Ramanujan wrote a few articles soon after he reached Cambridge. In June 1914, Hardy presented some of the results from Ramanujan's

Notebooks at a meeting of the London Mathematical Society. However, in January 1915, Ramanujan wrote to his friend S.M. Subramanian, that his "Notebook is sleeping in a corner for these four or five months". Ramanujan was obviously more interested in getting new results, and also partly due to the ongoing war, decided to publish the old results worked out in his Notebooks after the War. Though he did not live long enough to accomplish this.

After about an year and a half Hardy wrote to the Registrar of the University of Madras, that Ramanujan "is beyond question the best Indian mathematician of modern times … He will always be rather eccentric on his choice of subjects and methods of dealing with them … But of his extraordinary gifts there can be no questions; in some ways he is the most remarkable mathematician I have ever known".

This letter of Hardy and his Official Report to the University of Madras, along with an appeal by Sir Francis Spring to the University, in December 1915, to continue the assistance extended by it to Ramanujan, made the University extend the scholarship up to March 1919. During his five year stay in Cambridge, from April 1914 – March 1919, Ramanujan published 21 Research papers containing theorems on definite Integrals, Modular equations, Riemann's zeta function, Infinite series, Summation of series, Analytic Number theory, asymptotic formulae, Modular functions, Partitions, and Combinatorial Analysis.

His longest paper entitled 'Highly Composite Numbers' which appeared in the London Mathematical Society (LMS), in 1915, after it was abridged at the request of the Editors of the journal, is 62 pages long and it contains 269 equations. This is his longest paper.

The LMS had some financial difficulties at that time and Ramanujan was requested to reduce the length of his paper to save printing expenses. Five of these 21 research papers were in collaboration with his mentor Hardy. Ramanujan also published 5

Short Notes in the Records of the Proceedings at the meetings of the LMS and 6 more were in the Journal of the Indian Mathematical Society.

'The Collected Papers of Srinivasa Ramanujan', published in a volume running to 350 pages, was edited by G.H. Hardy, P.V. Seshu Iyer and

B.M. Wilson. The first edition of this book was published by the Cambridge University Press, in 1927, seven years after Ramanujan's death, resulted in a flurry of research papers by G.N. Watson (25 papers), C.T. Preece (6), W.N. Bailey (4), Robert A. Rankin (3) and some others during the period 1928 – 1938.

Town High School, Kumbakonam (Photo 2002).

Porter Hall, Kumbakonam (Photo 2002).

CHAPTER 5

Ramanujan's Graduation

Ramanujan was registered as a research student in June 1914 and the prerequisite of a diploma or a certificate, as the domiciliary requirement of six terms must have been relaxed in his extraordinary case.

Ramanujan was awarded the B.A. degree by Research, in March 1916, for his work on Highly Composite Numbers, along with six other publications and the thesis title bore the same name as that of his longest research paper. It is unfortunate that a copy of this dissertation is not to be found in the records of the University of Cambridge. According to Hardy, in his article in the 'Collected Papers of Ramanujan', this work of Ramanujan "is a very peculiar one, standing somewhat apart from the main channels of mathematical research. But the can be no question as to the extraordinary insight and ingenuity which he has shown in treating it, nor any doubt that the memoir is one of the most remarkable published in England for many years.

Ramanujan in convocation robes.

Ramanujan at the centre, on the Graduation day with the group.
(Hardy is at the extreme right.)

Ramanujan's designated tutor who monitored his progress at Trinity College, Cambridge, was E.W. Barnes, who considered Ramanujan as perhaps the most brilliant of all the top Trinity students, which included Littlewood (p. 233 of Kanigel's 'The Man who Knew Infinity'). Hardy was immensely satisfied with the progress of Ramanujan and wrote so to the Registrar of the University of Madras supporting an extension of Ramanujan's two year scholarship "… until, as I confidently expect, he is elected to a Fellowship at the College. Such an election I should expect in October 1917".

Later, in June 1916, in an official report on the progress of Ramanujan's work in England, to the Registrar of the University of Madras, Hardy wrote:

"… it is safe to say that Mr. Ramanujan has justified abundantly all hopes that were based upon his work in India, and has shown that he possesses powers as remarkable in their way as those of any living mathematician. …

"I have said enough, I hope, to give some idea of his astonishing individuality and power. India has produced many talented mathematicians in recent years, a number of whom have come to

Cambridge and attained high academic distinction. They will be the first to recognize that Mr. Ramanujan's work is of a different category".

In spite of the raging World War, which deprived Ramanujan of the center stage which he would otherwise have commanded with his brilliant research work in the midst of his peers, the confidence he kindled in Hardy was enough to win for him recognition and laurels very soon, but unfortunately, the first signs of his illness appeared in Ramanujan in the Spring of 1917.

Ramanujan wrote letters addressed to his mother, from Trinity College, Cambridge, in Tamil. In the letter to his mother, reproduced (on the next page, p. 57), Ramanujan wrote:

"Trinity College

17 – 11 – 1916.

Salutations to Ramanuja. Offering many salutations to his Mother, Ramanujan reporting. I am safe. Write about your safety. The letter written by you has reached me. Before that the letter by Thirunarayanan also reached. I have all the pickles with me. I am getting from the city tamarind and all other things. You don't have to send anything. Only the 'koozhu vadaam' (sun-dried spiced rice flour fries) which you sent me now need to be sent and nothing else. Last week they have closed my college. They will reopen by middle of January. I am comfortable here. Keep the house so that it is good and presentable. Do not keep the gutter as usual. Get it covered properly with stone slabs. I am comfortable here. The sons from our neighbouring houses have arrived and they have joined in a college nearby.

Yours

Ramanujan."

Ramanujan was very close to his mother and his facial features bear a resemblance to her. They shared many things in common. As a child he loved to play the traditional South Indian game of goats and tigers, by drawing lines on the floor (Four one foot long lines diverging from a point are drawn and four horizontal lines are drawn equidistant from the point to its end. On the grid so formed, two players use different identifiable pebbles or tiny stones as markers and play a game akin to Checkers). She would comb his long hair, plait it and tied it up into a tuft at the back of the head. (In the year 1914, when he had decided to go to England, he sent his wife and mother back to Kumbakonam, and had his tuft removed and his hair-cropped to the prevalent English hair-style with the hair parted a few inches to the left of the center.

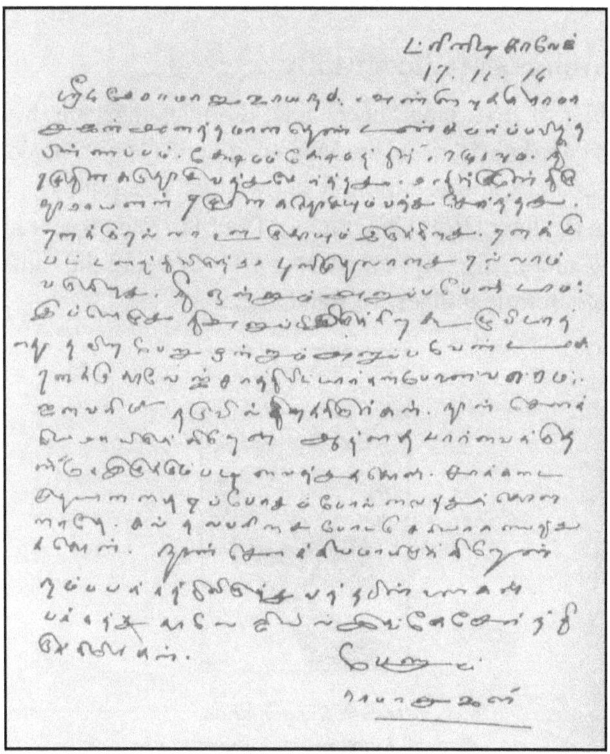

Ramanujan's letter, in Tamil, to his mother, from Cambridge, dated 17 November 1914.

The traditional caste mark would be placed on the forehead and even flowers would be placed in the tuft, when Ramanujan was a child. In fact, not to hurt her sentiments and feelings, Ramanujan sent her and his wife back to Kumbakonam, when they accompanied him on his long voyage to London from the Madras Harbour, before he followed the suggestions of Narayana Iyer to get his hair cut into the Western Crop and also learnt to wear trousers and he felt very uncomfortable to wear the shoes. He appeared in this attire for the first time before Professor Seshu Iyer whom he met in Madras, as he was also transferred from the Government Arts College to Presidency College, which fortunate circumstance, as stated earlier, resulted in Ramanujan discovering Hardy's "Orders of Infinity" book and starting his contact with him by writing his first letter to him in January 1914 and the rest is history.

Ramanujan's Medicography

Ramanujan's first biographer, S.R. Ranganathan, in his book, 'Ramanujan: The Man and the Mathematician' (1967), stated that by the end of 1918, it was definitely known that Tuberculosis (TB) had set in. In the later (1991) biography, 'The Man Who Knew Infinity', Robert Kanigel, also lays emphasis on TB as being the cause of the prolonged, terminal illness of Ramanujan.

Dr. S.R. Ranganathan.
(Shiyali Ramamritha Ranganathan)
The first Librarian of the University of Madras, to whom
Hardy entrusted the Notebooks of Raman

A systematic study of the details led the mathematician Robert A. Rankin, in his article 'Ramanujan as a patient' (in the Proceedings of the Indian Academy of Sciences, Mathematics, vol. 93 (1984) 79 – 100) to point out that Ramanujan's illness was not properly diagnosed and TB was not the cause of his death. It is a fact that the warmer climate of Madras and its surroundings did not show any marked improvement in the health of Ramanujan. On the other hand, his health steadily deteriorated despite the best medical attention that was bestowed on him.

Robert A. Rankin, Scottish mathematician.

Ramanujan returned to India as a mathematician recognized from his brilliance by Hardy and the Western world and a celebrity. Towards the end, he was reduced to 'to only skin and bone', as described by his wife Janakiammal, who along with Ramanujan's mother Komalathammal, vied with each other to attend to the needs of Ramanujan and to look after his declining health.

Dr. D.A.B. Young, in 1990s, researched into the illness of Ramanujan, and in his article entitled, 'Ramanujan's illness', gives us a better insight into the health of Ramanujan. Given here is a brief summary of this medical biography, which we term as medicography!

Ramanujan came to Madras in 1906, joined the Pachaiyappa's College to study in the F.A. class again. Unfortunately, within a few months of his stay at the Victoria Hostel, in Triplicane, he fell ill with dysentery and had to return to Kumabkonam for a period of about three months. It is conjectured by Dr. Young, after sieving through all the information, that Ramanujan's dysentery was caused by amoebiasis, a tropical infection, widespread in the metropolitan cities of India.

"Amoebiasis, unless adequately treated, is a permanent infection, although many patients may go for long periods with no overt signs of the disease. Relapses occur when the host-parasite relationship is disturbed. Ramanujan experienced such a relapse, I believe, in 1909, when according to his friend R.R. Ayyar (in S.R.Ranganathan's biography):

'Ramanujan who was living in [Madras], became seriously ill … As a patient … he was obstinate and would not drink hot water and insisted on eating grapes which were sour and bad for him. [The doctor] after examining him, asked me to send him to his parents as his condition required constant nursing'. How ill Ramanujan felt at this time is indicated by his giving his host for safe keeping the two large Notebooks kept with him all the time d and in which he had been recording his mathematical results; the same Notebooks that are now famous as a major legacy of his genius. …

"Later the same year (1909), while still at home with his family, he developed a hydrocele, which was operated on in January 1910. … … Dr. Shaw's suspicion that the operation was the excision of a malignant growth, depending as it must have done on Ramanujan's exact description of the lesion, certainly favours the explanation of a scrotal amoeboma rather than a hydrocele".

These were the illnesses suffered by Ramanujan before and after his marriage to Janaki, in 1909. and before his departure to England. From all accounts available it appears that his health was reasonably good during the first three years of his stay in Cambridge, despite his strict vegetarian diet, the food shortages and his own 'cooking only once a day or two'. This was also his most productive period in Cambridge. From May 1917, when he was first admitted to the Nursing Hostel in Cambridge for 5 months, he seems to have been in and out of TB Sanatoria – Mendip Hills in Somerset (for 2 - 3 weeks in October 1917), Matlock House in Derbyshire (where he was from November 1917 – June 1918); Fitzroy House in London (from June to December 1918) and Colinette House, Putney (till end of December 1918) – until his departure to India in March 1919.

Kanchipuram temple, where Ramanujan had his initiation
to 3 R's: 'Aksharabhyasam'.

Symptoms of improvement showed, after considerable treatment for tuberculosis, in the autumn of 1918. he was able to meet all his medical expenses incurred during his illness out of his earning accumulated through frugal living. Thanks to the unstinted efforts of Hardy, who did his best to get Ramanujan due recognition, he was elected a Fellow of the Royal Society of London in February 1918. Reproduced here, is a note of Littlewood on this subject:

Littlewood's note on Ramanujan's Fellowship Election (1918)

"I am the only person who knows the facts, by letter and they should be put on record. If only as illustrating the fantastic state of the College just after the 1914-1918 war, when there were only the unfit, and people over military age, mostly ferocious Huns. I don't see why I should suppress names.

"There was much opposition. Hardy was not made an Elector and I acted, by letter, because I was quite ill (after concussion on the top of Years without proper holidays from hard work).

"I did get wind of the Enemy's tactics from R.A. Herman, who was a close personal friend, and although he was again Ramanujan himself, he was always naively honest.

"I said: 'You can't reject an F.R.S. Yes, we though that was a dirty trick! I gathered also (i) that R.V. Laurence had been saying that he wasn't going to have a black man as a Fellow;

J.E. Littlewood, M.A.

G.H. Hardy, M.A.

"(ii) that 'grave doubts' were being expressed about his mental state.

"I met this last by getting two doctor's certificates. I spoke to E. Harrison, who was pro-Ramanujan, but not an Elector; he was obviously worried.

"At the actual Election, he was elected, I don't know what majority; But it was decided that the doctor's certificates should not be read.

– (sd.) J.E. Littlewood".

Reproduced here is an excerpt from the Records of the Royal Society, dated 18 December 1917, a copy of which is an exhibit in the Ramanujan Museum, at Royapuram, Madras, in the Avvai Kalai Kazhagam.

Certificate for a Candidate for Election.

Name and Title or Designation Profession	Srinivasa Ramanujan Research Student in Mathematics
Usual Place of Residence	Trinity College, Cambridge

Qualifications (Not to exceed 250 words):

Distinguished as a pure mathematician, particularly for his investigations in elliptic functions and the theory of numbers. Author of the following papers, amongst others: 'Modular equations and approximations to p', Quarterly Journal, vol. 45; 'New expressions of Riemann's functions V(s) and X(t)', ibid, vol. 46; 'Highly composite numbers', Proc. London. Math. Soc., vol. 14; 'On certain arithmetical functions', Trans. Camb. Phil. Soc. Vol. 22; 'On the expression of a number in the form $ax2 + by2 + cz2 + dt2$,' Proc. Camb. Phil. Soc., vol. 19. Joint author with G.H. Hardy, F.R.S., of the following papers: 'Une formulae asymptotique poour le nombre des partitions de n', Comptes Rendus, 2 Jan. 1917; 'Asymptotic Formulae for the distribution of numbers of various types', Proc.London Math. Soc., vol. 16; 'The normal number of prime factors of a number n', Quarterly Journal, vol. 47; 'Asymptotic Formulae *in Combinatory Analysis', Proc. London Math. Soc. (awaiting publication).*

Being desirous of admission into the ROYAL SOCIETY OF LONDON, we the undersigned propose and recommend him as deserving that honour, and as likely to become a useful and valuable member.

From General knowledge.   From Personal Knowledge.

(sd.) E.T. Whittaker	(sd.) G.H. Hardy *Proposer.*
(sd.) A.R. Forsyth	(sd.) P.A. MacMahon *Seconder.*
(sd.) A.N. Whitehead	(sd.) J.H. Grace
	(sd.) Joseph Larmor
	(sd.) T.J.I'A. Bromwich
	(sd.) E.W. Hobson
	(sd.) H.F. Baker
	(sd.) J.E. Littlewood
	(sd.) J.W. Nicolson

Suspended for 1918.

This certificate on a printed form of the Royal Society has been filled by hand (and the hand writing appears to be that of Mr. Hardy). The citation awarding the Fellowship of Royal Society to Ramanujan read:

"Srinivasa Ramanujan, Trinity College, Cambridge. Research student in Mathematics Distinguished as a pure mathematician particularly for his investigations in elliptic functions and the theory of numbers".

The renowned Physicist, Professor R.H. Dalitz, Oxford University, on his visit to the Institute of Mathematical Sciences, in February 1966, spent some time with me discussing the various aspects concerning Sir C.V. Raman and Srinivasa Ramanujan, the two giants of Indian Science.

S. Chandrasekhar ('Chandra') was a personal friend of Professor Dalitz. After he returned to Oxford we had several interesting exchanges and in an e-mail this is what he wrote about Ramanujan's F.R.S.:

Dr. R .H. Dalitz   **Dr. S. Chandrasekhar, NL.**

"I did not succeed in finding Ramanujan's signature in the Royal Society book. The book is indexed, so it is just not there. The reason is undoubtedly is that he was ill in that period and could not go to the Royal Society to sign it. There are other examples of well-known FRS's who somehow didn't get their signature into the book. That means that he did not ever attend any meeting of the Royal Society; if he had, ey would have brought out the book and not let him go until he had signed. Of course, it was also war time, which meant that there were as few meetings as possible".

Ramanujan was elected to a Trinity College Fellowship, in October 1918, which was a Prize Fellowship worth £250 a year for six years with no duties or conditions. These awards acted as great incentives to Ramanujan who discovered some of the most beautiful theorems in mathematics, subsequently.

Hardy's letter to the Registrar of the University of Madras, Mr. Dewsbury , dated November 26, 1918, struck a hopeful note:

"There is at last, I am profoundly glad to say, a quite definite change for the better. I think we may now hope that he has turned the corner, and is on the road to recovery.

"His temperature has ceased to be irregular, and he has gained nearly a stone in weight. The consensus of medical opinion is that he has been suffering from some obscure source of blood poisoning, which has now dried up; and that it is reasonable to expect him to recover his health completely and if all goes well rapidly."

The New Court, Trinity College, where Hardy lived when Ramanujan had his five year sojourn in Cambridge (Feb. 1914 – March 1919).

Ramanujan's symptoms were predominantly night-time fever, loss of weight leading to his emaciated looks and these caused depressions which once drove him to the limit of attempting suicide – a story recounted many years after his death by Dr. S. Chandrasekhar as told to him by Professor Hardy (as recounted earlier). These symptoms made the doctors consider various diagnosis, at different times, such as: gastric ulcer, malaria, typhoid, tuberculosis, cancer of the liver, etc. In recent times, with hindsight, vitamin B-12 deficiency (something unknown to the world at that time) has been diagnosed as a possibility, by

Dr. D.A.B. Young, in his article entitled: "Ramanujan's illness", in Current Science, vol. 67 (1994) pages 967 – 972.

The recovery alluded to by Hardy in his letter to Dewsbury was obviously the reason why Ramanujan was persuaded to return to India, with the hope that he would soon recover and return to take up the Trinity College Fellowship awarded to him for five years.

L to R: Dr. B.D. Acharya, Author K.S.R., President of India Dr. A.P.J.Abdul Kalam, Dr. V.S.Ramamurthy (Sec., DST) and Mrs. Rajeswari Ramaurthy.

Presented the CD Roms to the President of India, Dr. A.P.J. Abdul Kalamon Dec. 26, 2005 at the Rashtrapathi Bahvan, along Dr. B.D.Acharya, Head Mathematics Division, Department of Science and Technology.

CHAPTER 6

The beginning of the end

After completing nearly five years at Cambridge, early in 1919, when Ramanujan appeared to have recovered sufficiently to withstand the rigours of a long voyage to India, he left England on February 27, 1919, by s.s. Nagoya. Four weeks later on March 27, he arrived at Bombay port and soon after at Madras, by rail, thin, pale and emaciated, but "with a scientific standing and reputation such as no Indian has enjoyed before". Professor Hardy who expressed this view (in a letter to the Registrar of the Madras University, Dewsbury) also hoped that "India will regard him as the treasure he is". Hardy urged the Madras University to make a permanent provision for Ramanujan to enable him to continue his research work. Again the University of Madras rose to the occasion by granting him £250 a year as allowance for five years, commencing from April 1919. Ramanujan was sent back to India by Hardy with the hope that the warmer climate and the family atmosphere would help his complete recovery from tuberculosis.

Most unfortunately, his precarious health did not improve on his return to India. Fever relapsed and in addition, Janaki recalled that he suffered severe bouts of stomach ache.

Ramanujan was subjected to fits of depression, had a premonition of his death and was generally considered a difficult patient.

Ramanujan spent three months in Madras, two months in Kodumudi, and four months in Kumbakonam. When his condition showed signs of further deterioration, after great persuasion, Ramanujan was brought to Madras for expert medical treatment, in January 1920.

Despite all the tender attention he could get from his wife who nursed him throughout this period, and the best medical attention from the doctors, his untimely end came on April 26, 1920, at 'Gometra' the residence of Emperumal Chettiar, a philanthropist, in Chetput, Madras, when Ramanujan was 32 Years, 4 Months and 4 days old.

From all the available evidence and retrospective diagnosis, Dr. Young makes out the cause for the terminal illness of Ramanujan as hepatic amoebiasis, a tropical disease contacted by Ramanujan for the first time in 1906. Young reasons why this was not diagnosed at that time and it is best to recount this in his own words:

"Hepatic amoebiasis was regarded in 1918 as a tropical disease ('tropical liver abscess'), and this would have had important implications for successful diagnosis, especially in provincial medical centers.

Furthermore, the specialists called in were experts in either tuberculosis or gastric medicine. Another major difficulty is that a patient with this disease would not, unless specifically asked, recall as relevant that he had had two episodes of dysentery 11 and 8 years before.

'Gometra', Chetpet, Madras. A bungalow of Namperumal Chettiar,,where Ramanujan breathed his last, at 10 A.M., on April 26, 1920.

"Finally, there is the very good reason that, because of the great variability in physical findings, the diagnosis was difficult in 1918 and remains as today: hepatic amoebiasis 'presents a severe challenge to the diagnostic skills … [and] should be considered in any patient with fever and an abnormal abdominal examination coming from an endemic area'."

Hardy, who was expecting to hear about the recovery of Ramanujan after his return to India, was unaware that the end was to come so soon and so he was naturally shocked when the news came to him from Madras in a letter. It is relevant to quote what Hardy wrote years later in his classic book 'A Mathematician's Apology' (1940):

"Galois did at twenty-one, Abel at twenty-seven, Ramanujan at thirty-three, Riemann at forty … I do not know an instance of a major mathematical advance initiated by a man past fifty."

However, we may site a few examples which explode the myth of the Young Mathematician are: Newton's 'Principia' which was written when Newton was in his mid forties; Euler, despite his blindness, produced his three volumes on integral calculus when he was in his sixties; Gauss at 34 proposed his theory of analytic functions; and, in more recent times, Cartan, Poincare, Siegel, Kolmogorov and Erdos exhibited creativity in mathematics in their later years" – ref. Susan Landau, Notices of the American Mathematical Society, vol. 44 (1997) 1284.

Janaki Ramanujan: the woman behind the genius

Janaki was born on March 21, 1899. She was the fourth daughter and one of six children (fice daughters and a son) of Rangaswamy Iyengar and Rnaganayaki Ammal of Rajendram village, close to Marudur Railway station. Janaki's mother was a friend of Ramanujna's mother, Komalathammal, who on a visit to Rajendram saw the pretty nine year old girl and negotiated with the parents of Janaki to get Janaki married to her son Ramanujan, who was 21 years old at that time. The marriage took place on July 14, 1909. Rmanujan's father was not present at the wedding. A delay in the arrival of Ramanujan with his mother on the day of the wedding was the cause for anxiety to the parents of Janaki, who even though of another groom for Janaki, to avoid the stigma to the family that the marriage did not take place as planned!

The Ramanujan – Janaki wedding was a traditional five-day ceremony and it took place along with the wedding of another sister of Janaki.

After the wedding, Komalathammal took Janaki along with her son to Kumabkonam. The young wife was soon back with her parents. She came of age and joined Ramanujan in 1912, after Ramanujan got a clerical post in the Madras Port Trust, thanks to the efforts of Narayana Iyer, then the Treasurer of Port Trust. The monthly salary of Ramanujan was Rs. 30. They resided at Saiva Muthiah (Mudali) Street, in George Town. In May 1913, Ramanujan joined the University of Madras as its first research scholar and for about ten months he moved to Hanumantha Rayan Koil Street and then to Thoppu Venkatachala (Mudali) Street, both in Triplicane. His wife and mother lived with him for some months at the latter residence, before he left for England, on March 17, 1914.

Janaki - young widow

Janaki ammal - in her oldage.

Ramanujan was alone in England for almost five years (April 14, 1914 to February 27, 1919) and he fell ill in the Spring of 1917. He was diagnosed and treated for Tuberculosis, which at that time was considered a contagious disease, and the patients were isolated and confined in special Sanatoria.

The ongoing first World War prevented the possibility of his wife joining him to take care of him or his being shifted to a warmer country like Italy (thought of as a possible destination by Hardy). Eventually, after the war ended, Ramanujan returned to India in April 1919, emaciated from the prolonged confinement, (for nearly half of his five year sojourn in England), but with a repuatation and to a rousing reception, when Komalathammal, Narayana Iyer, Kasturiranga Iyengar (the founder of the Hindu newspaper) and others went to receive him on his arrival at the docks in Bombay. Ramanujan was disappointed that Janaki was not there as a part of the grand reception committee. Janaki joined him and lived with him in Madras, when the best medical attention was bestowed on Ramanujan, who returned with a B.A. degree of Cambridge University, and as the first coveted elected Fellow of the Royal Society of London, he had the status of a reputed mathematician and a celebrity.

The parental joint family home was run, during that period, by Ramanujan's mother Komalathammal and his grandmother Ranganayakiammal. In later years, after the untimely death of Ramanujan at 10 A.M. of April 26, 1920, Janaki stated happily (to the author who was accompanying Bruce Berndt) that:

"I considered it my good fortunate to give him rice, lemon juice, butter milk, etc. at regular intervals and to give fomentation to his legs and chest when he reported pain. The two vessels used then for preparing bot water are alone with me; these remind me often of those days."

After April 1920, the young widow spent the next eight years of her life in Bombay, with her brother, R.S. Iyengar, who was an Assistant Commissioner of Income Tax. During that period, she learnt tailoring and English language at home. IN 1931, without any resources – having been deprived of all her dowry ('sthree dhanam') – she returned to Madras and spent a year with one of her sisters and another year with friends, before deciding to live independently. She started to teach tailoring and lived in a small house in Hanumantharaya Koil Street, in Triplicane, having one room downstairs and one room upstairs, for the next five decades. She earned enough from her suturing of dresses for girls and ladies, and could even save a little, thanks to her frugal living. IN 1950, one of her friends, Soundaravalli, died suddenly entrusting her with her 7 year-old son, W. Narayanan.

Janakiammal took up the responsibility of bringing up this boy and became his foster mother. During his school years (1952 - 1955), Narayanan was sent by Janaki to the Sri Ramakrishna Mission Boarding School. She educated him up to the Bachelor's Degree in Commerce (B.Com) of the University of Madras, in Vivekananda College, Madras. She approached the Port Trust Chairman and secured for Narayanan, a clerical post in the State Bank of India. Janakiammal conducted the marriage of her foster son, in 1972, after she selected Vaidehi, also an employee of the State Bank of India, in 1972. To take care of Janakiammal, Narayanan and Vaidehi denied themselves the promotions, so that they could remain in Madras. Eventually Narayanan took voluntary retirement from the Bank, in 1988, and this enabled him and his wife to devote all their attention on the aging Janakiammal for the next 6 years.

The Narayanans have a son and two daughters and the family took good care of Janakiammal and she on her part contributed in every possible way to their well-being and education at Schools and colleges – N. Sridhar is now a C.A., I.C.W.A., N. Sripriya is an M.C.A. and N. Sri Vidya is a B.Com. and all are well-settled in life now.

Being extremely orthodox and pious, Janakiammal preferred to stay alone in her house in Muthiah Mudali II Street, Triplicane, under the loving and tender care of Vaidehi and Narayanan, till a few years before her demise, when she moved to 14, Hanumantharayan Koil Street, also in Triplicane. This house was purchased by Janakiammal with her savings.

Philanthropic and sympathetic by nature, Janakiammal supported financially the education of several children and youngsters. T. Rama-swami (father of the renowned guitarist Prasanna), was also one of the young men who was educated by her, along with Narayanan. Some parents used to go to her and request her for token amounts towards their child's school fees, since they considered it auspicious to get her kind words of support and blessings for success.

Janakiammal was receiving a Pension from the University of Madras since 1920, the year of Ramanujan's death. This amount which was only Rs. 20 per month at that time, gradually rose to about Rs. 300 per month.

In interviews which appeared in newspapers, soon after the 'Lost' Notebook of Ramanujan was discovered by George Andrews, in 1976, Janakiammal lamented that even a bust of Ramanujan was not made, although one had been promised. Professor Richard A. Askey, a renowned mathematician at University of Wisconsin, saw these newspaper interviews and decided that a bust of Ramanujan was long

overdue since Ramanujan's widow wanted one, and that "In Ramanujan's case a permanent memorial is appropriate: one which can be appreciated by those who do not understand his mathematics should be added to the memorial Ramanujan made for himself with his work." So, garnering the support of about a hundred mathematicians, including Professors George Andrews, Bruce Berndt and S. Chandrasekhar, Professor Askey commissioned a bronze bust, from the only authentic passport size photograph of Ramanujan, by Paul Grunlund, sculptor-in-charge at the Gustavus Adolphous College at Saint Peter, Minnesota in U.S.A. A copy of this bust was presented to Mrs. Janaki Ramanujan in 1985, at a formal function in the University of Madras.

Besides the original presented to Janakiammal on the occasion of the Birth Centenary of Ramanujan, ten copies were made. These are now at: Raman Research Institute, Tata Institute of Fundamental Research, Indian Academy of Sciences, Inter University Consortium for Astronomy and Astrophysics, Ministry of Defense, Cambridge University Library, the Royal Society London, Vaughn Museum and two in private collections.

Janakiammal had cherished memories of her great husband. Even in recent years, though she was hard of hearing, had failing eyesight and was having indifferent health, when mathematicians, like Professors George E. Andrews, Bruce C. Berndt, Richard A. Askey and Bela Bollobas, made it a point to call on her to call on her to pay their respects to the living spouse the mathematical genius, she used to recall with pride the prophetic words of her husband that his mathematics will provide for her, irrespective of whether he was alive or dead.

Bust of Ramanujan, sculpted by Paul Grunlund, 1985.

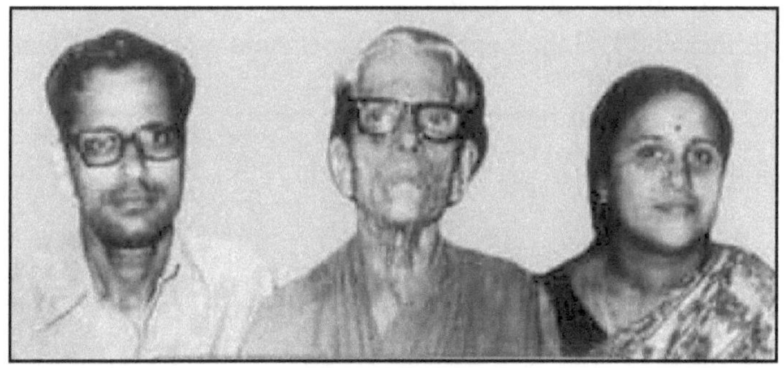

W. Narayanan, Janakiammal and Vaidehi Narayanan.

She also pointed out that on such occasions, when asked, that recognition and financial support started coming to her after the 75th birth anniversary celebrations of Ramanujan, in 1962. On that occasion, a commemorative stamp and a first day cover were released by the Indian Philately Association, Government of India.

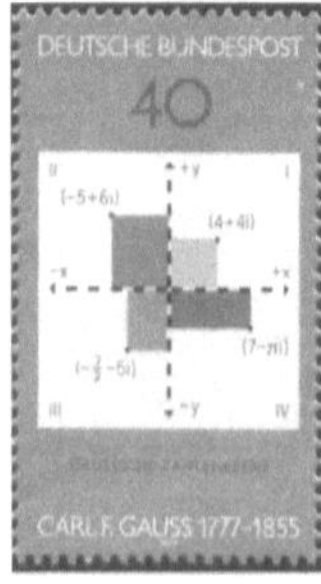

Note: Most countries have the tradition of honouring their great scientists by bringing out on special occasions Commemorative Stamps and First Day Covers.

The Federal Republic of Germany issued a Stamp and the ten Deutsch Mark currency note in honour of Carl Friedrich Gauss (1777 - 1855). On the stamp, the Gaussian complex number is depicted. A Gaussian complex number is defined as: $x + i y$, x and y being integers. $2 = (1+ i) (1- i)$, and $5 = (1+2i) (1- 2i)$ or $(2+i)(2- i)$ are composite Gaussian numbers, while 3 is a Gaussian prime number. Gauss proved the unique factorization theorem for these integers and primes and laid the foundation for Algebraic Number Theory.

The March 1998 issue of the Notices of the American Mathematical Society (Volume 45, No.3) carries on its cover A Collection of Mathematical stamps – of Ramanujan, Bolzano, Lagrange, Pascal, Kovalevsakaya, al-Khwarizmi, Dedekind, Newton and Cauchy. The fact that the first of these stamps was chosen as that of Ramanujan, is indicative of the world recognition to this untutored natural genius. While there exists a Stamp Corner column in the Mathematical Intelligencer, the author is unaware of one such for Currency Notes!

Cover page of the Notices of the AMS, March 1998.

During the Centenary Year of the Madras Port Trust, Janakiammal was honoured and was given a Pension for life. Since then, monthly pernsions were also offered to her by the Governments of Tamilnadu,

Andhra Pradesh and West Bengal, the Indian National Science Academy, the Ramanujan Mathematical Society (founded in 1985) and by the Hindujan Foundation (London).

Mr. A.P. Venkateswaran, the Secreatry of the Hinduja Foundation, at the instance of Professor E.C.G. Sudarshan, Director of the Institute of Mathematical Sciences, Madras, was instrumental in presenting a purse of Rs. 20,000 to Janakiammal, from the funds of the Hinduja Foundation. An honorarium of Rs. 1000 per month was also announced, at this function, organized by the author, at the Institute of Mathematical Sciences premises, at a simple, solemn function, on August 13, 1987, with the Hon'ble Minister, Mr. C. Subramanaiam, the Patron of MATSCIENCE, presiding over the function. Janakiammal came to the venue of the meeting, on the campus of the Institute of Mathematical Sciences, accompanied by her foster son W. Narayanan with his wife, Mrs. Vaidehi Narayanan and other relatives.

Even during those months of prolonged illness, Ramanujan kept on working, though he was not in a position to sit up, at a furious pace and kept jotting down his discoveries on sheets of paper, nursed by Janaki who used to offer food to him. These 138 sheets were found in a box years later, in 1976, by George E. Andrews, in the archives of Trinity College, when he was looking into the estate of G.N. Watson. These are referred to as the 'Lost' Notebook of Ramanujan today (and more about this later).

Janakiammal had cherished memories of her great husband. Even in recent years, though she was hard of hearing, had failing eye sight and was having indifferent heath, when I accompanied mathematicians like Professors Andrews, Askey, Berndt, Bollabos and others, who wanted to call on her at her residence, she recalled with pride the prophetic words of her husband that his mathematics would provide for her whether he was alive or dead. She also pointed out on such occasions, when asked, that recognition and financial support to her started coming after the 75th Birth Anniversary celebrations of Ramanujan in 1962, the year in which a commemorative stamp and a first day cover were brought out by the Government of India. During the centenary year of the Madras Port Trust, she was honoured and was given a pension for life. Since then, the Governments of Tamilnadu, Andhra Pradesh and West Bengal, the Indian National Science Academy, the Ramanujan Mathematical Society (founded in 1985) and the Hinduja Foundation were also giving her monthly pensions.

Janakiammal, honoured at a function.

Janakiammal Ramanujan, the wife of Srinivasa Ramanujan, acclaimed as the greatest mathematician of the twentieth century, during the last year of life, was ailing with natural aging problems. She would not permit anyone other than her foster son W. Narayanan to help her with her daily chores. She insisted and persisted in cooking food for herself almost till her final days. As a dutiful son, Narayanan and his wife, took voluntary retirement, from the State Bank of India, to take care of the aging Janakiammal. Since she was hard of hearing, and found the use of hearing-aids more disturbing than useful (since they would amplify not only the signal but the noises also), whenever questions were posed to her by the visitors, Narayanan would shout the question posed, in Tamil, into her ear and she, in turn, would reply, often in a clear, loud voice. When I accompanied a visiting Professor, who hesitatingly asked her whether she had conjugal relationship with her husband – since she got married at 9, and lived together with him only for about a year before he left for Cambridge, and again for a little more than a year, ailing with suspected Tuberculosis after he returned – Janakiammal's face had a beaming smile and she answered in the affirmative.

Janakiammal breathed her last on the morning of April 13, 1994, at her residence, which she had purchased out of her own savings: 14, Hanumantharayan Koil Street, Triplicane, at the age of 94. She lived for seven decades after Ramanujan died. Narayanan called me and informed me as soon as the doctor had pronounced her death, and I paid my last respects to Janakiammal, in the traditional manner, with a garland of flowers placed respectfully at her feet and praying silently for a few minutes for her soul to rest in peace.

Statue at Ramanujan IT City, Taramani sculpted by A.Ravi.

CHAPTER 7

Human qualities in Ramanujan

The physical features of Ramanujan as recorded by Professor E.H. Neville, in a letter to Dewsbury, the Registrar of the University of Madras: "In figure he was a little below medium height (5 ft. 5 in.) and stout until emaciated by disease; he had a big head, with long black hair brushed sideways above a big forehead; his face was square, he was clean shaven and his complexion never really dark, grew paler during his life in England; his ears were small, his nose broad, and always his shining eyes were the conspicuous feature that Ramachandra Rao observed in 1910. He walked stiffly, with head erect and toes out-turned; if he was not talking as he walked, his arms were held clear of the body, with hands open and palms downwards. But when he talked, whether he was walking or standing, sitting or lying down, his slender fingers were for ever alive, as eloquent as his countenance".

Ramanujan had only one passion in life – mathematics. He devoted all his time to this subject and its development. Quoting Professor Neville again, from P.K. Srinivasan's: 'Ramanujan: Letters and Reminiscences', had:

"an instinctive perfection of manners that made him a delightful guest or companion. Success and fame left his natural simplicity quite untouched. To his friends he was devoted beyond measure, and he devised curiously personal ways of showing his gratitude and expressing his affection. The wonderful mathematician was indeed a lovable man".

This is in complete accord with the views of Hardy on Ramanujan:

"… the picture I want to present to you is that of a man who had his peculiarities like other distinguished men, but a man in whose society one could take pleasure, with whom one could drink tea and discuss politics, or mathematics; the picture in short, not of a wonder from the East, or an inspired idiot, or a psychological fraud, but of a rational human being who happened to be a great mathematician".

The integrity of Ramanujan is transparent from the following statement of Hardy (a footnote in the 'Collected papers of Ramanujan', on p. xxxiii):

"All of Ramanujan's manuscripts passed through my hands, and I edited them very carefully for publication. The earlier ones I wrote completely. I had no share of any kind in the results, except of course when I was actually a collaborator, or when explicit acknowledgement was made. Ramanujan was almost absurdly scrupulous in his desire to acknowledge the slightest help."

Group Photograph after the award of B.A. degree by research of the Cambridge University to Ramanujan, in March 1916.

In a letter to a friend of Ramanujan, S.M. Subramanian, Hardy wrote, in September 1917, that:

Ramanujan "has been seriously ill but is now a good deal better. It is very difficult to get him to take proper care of himself; if he would only do so we should have every hope that he would be quite well again before very long".

And that Ramanujan "was not writing to his people nor apparently hearing from them. He was very reserved about it and it appeared to us that there must have been some quarrel". Hardy expressed his anxiety regarding the trouble which might have arisen and wanted it to be cleared anyway.

Ramanujan was shy by temperament and contemplative by nature. He was a man with a great sense of humour. He punned on the word Tanjavur by splitting this word into three words:'than' +'chavu'+ 'voor', which mean 'his'+'death'+'town' and wanted to be shifted from that city. "He had a fund of stories, and such was his enjoyment in telling them that in his great days his irrepressible laughter often swallowed the climax of his narrative", stated Neville, in his article. He was very affectionate towards his two younger brothers and his mother, in particular.

Janaki recollected that Ramanujan knew astrology and made astrological predictions to some extent. Because of this ability, he knew that he would not live beyond 34 years and he is supposed to have made predictions for others also.

Some friends of Ramanujan, T.K. Rajagopalan, R. Srinivasan and R. Radhakrishnan Ayyar, remembered that Ramanujan could foresee events in visions; that being an ardent devotee of Lord Narasimha, he saw drops of blood from the God's teeth falling, as a sign of the Lord's grace, and "after seeing such drops, scrolls containing the most complicated mathematics used to unfold before him, and these he set down on paper on waking only a fraction what was shown to him".

Ramanujan's maternal grandmother was a staunch devotee of Goddess Namagiri or Namakkal. Ramanujan himself was known to his friends to be a devotee of the Goddess of Namakkal and he used to say that the Goddess appeared in his dreams and inspired him to come forth with new formulae.

This was probably Ramanujan's only way of explaining away his incomparable intuition and discoveries of new mathematical theorems, to those who could not comprehend his ability to churn out continuously new results but who persisted in questioning him as to how he arrived at those results!

Presiding Deity:
Sri Lakshminarasimha

'Uthsavar': Goddess
Namagiri of Namakkal

Professor K. Ananda Rao was at King's College, when Ramanujan was at Trinity College, and he recalled, (PKS, vol. I, in 1962, p. 143 – 144) that: "In his nature, he was simple, entirely free from affectation, with no trace whatever of his being self-conscious of his abilities. He was quite sociable, very polite and considerate to others".

Ramanujan never forgot that as a first born to his parents, he had to shoulder the responsibility of taking care of his parents. He was compassionate. Accepting the Madras University offer of a scholarship, he wrote to Dewsbury, the Registrar of the University, in his letter dated January 11, 1919, from a Nursing Home in Putney:

"I feel, however, that after my return to India, which I expect to happen as soon as arrangements can be made, the total amount of money to which I shall be entitled will be much more than I shall require. I should hope that, after my expenses in England have been paid, £50 a year will be paid to my parents and that the surplus, after my necessary expenses are met, should be used for some educational purpose, such in particular as the reduction of school-fees, for poor boys and orphans and provision of books in schools. No doubt it will be possible to make an arrangement about this after my return. ... I feel very sorry that, as I have not been well, I have not been able to do so much mathematics during the last two years as before. I hope that I shall soon be able to do more and will certainly do my best to deserve the help that has been given to me."

Ramanujan concluded a letter to Narayana Iyer, in November 1915, from Cambridge, with the following words of gratitiude: "I am ever indebted to you and Sir Francis Spring for your zealous interest in my case from the very beginning of acquaintance".

In January 1920, Ramanujan in his last and only letter to Hardy after his return to India, communicated his discovery of what he called as 'mock' theta functions, a subject of considerable interest for research workers today. Ramanujan wote:

"I am extremely sorry for not writing to you a single letter up to now. ...

"I discovered very interesting functions recently which I call Mock theta-functions. Unlike the False theta-functions (studied partially by Prof. L.J. Rogers in his interesting paper) they enter into mathematics as beautifully as the ordinary theta-functions. I am sending with this letter some examples..."

The classical one-dimensional Heat equation and the Kortweg - de Vries equation have been solved in terms of theta functions. In recent times, theta functions have been found to be of great use in the theory of Solitons – a field of great interest in modern theoretical Phyiscs.

Freeman J. Dyson, a renowned theoretical physicist, on the occasion of the Ramanujan Birth Centenary – in 'Ramanujan Revisted', edited by George E. Andrews, et. al. – stated:

"My dream is that I will live to see the day when young physicists, struggling to bring the predictions of superstring theory into correspondence with the facts of nature, will be led to enlarge their analytic machinery to include not only theta-functions, but also mock theta-functions."

Freeman J. Dyson, Institute for Advanced Study, Princeton.

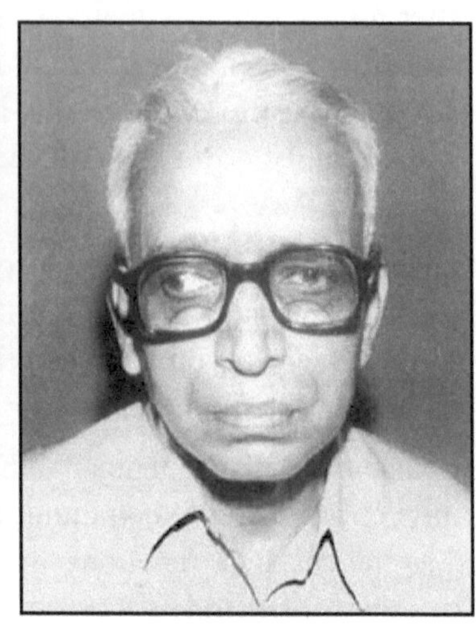

K.G. Ramanathan, Tata Institute of Fundamental Research, Bombay.

It is Ramanujan's results on continued fractions, contained in his first historic letter to Hardy, in January 1913, which made Hardy state that the formulae 'defeated' him completely.

Ramanujan's major work on continued fractions revolves around the generalization of what is called today as the Ramanujan continued fraction:

$$C(x) = \cfrac{1}{1 + \cfrac{x}{1 + \cfrac{x^2}{1 + \cfrac{x^3}{1 + \ldots}}}} \quad \text{for } |x| < 1. \quad (1.1.1)$$

$$= 1\,/\,1 + (\,x\,/\,1 + (x2\,/\,1 + (x3\,/\,1 + (\ldots))))), |x| < 1.$$

K.G. Ramanathan, the renowned mathematician of the Tata Institute of Fundamental Research, Bombay in his Homi J. Bhabha medal Lecture -1984 Entitled: Ramanujan's continued fraction, stated:

"This continued fraction was, however, first discovered by L.J. Rogers in his beautiful work 'Second memoir on the exponent of certain infinite products', (in the proceedings of the London Mathematical Soc., Vol. 25 (1894) 318 –343), on expansions of infinite products. It was rediscovered around 1911 by Ramanujan who recognized its importance and applied to it the methods of elliptic and modula functions. Indeed, in his, now famous, first letter to Hardy in 1913, he stated a number of beautiful results about (1.1.1) which led Hardy to believe, and rightly too, that these could have been written down only by a mathematician of the highest class. In the 'Lost' note book, he gave a number of generalizations of (1.1.1) and their evaluation at points in an imaginary quadratic field.

"Atle Selberg, in 1936, (in the article:'Über einige arithmetische Identitäten', Avhand. Utigitt. Norske Vid. Akad. Oslo (1936) No.8, 23p.), working independently, rediscovered almost all of Ramanujan's generalizations of (1.1.1) and the Rogers – Ramanujan identities. Some of Schur's results on (1.1.1) are also found in the 'Lost' note book."

Atle Selberg (1917 – 2007), the Norwegian mathematician is renowned for his work in Analytic Number theory and automorphic forms and their relation to Spectral theory, won the highest honour in mathematics of being awarded the Fields Medal in the year 1950. "While he was still at school he was influenced by the work of Srinivasa Ramanujan and he discovered the exact analytical formula for the partition function as suggested by the works of Ramanujan", (which was first published by Hans Rademacher). Selberg, in his 'Reflections Around the Ramanujan Centenary' (reproduced in 'Resonance', December 1996), at the Tata Institute of Fundamental Research, in Bombay, observed that:

"a felicitous but unproved conjecture may be of much more consequence for mathematics than the proof of many a respectable theorem.

"Ramanujan's recognition of the multiplicative properties of the coefficients of modular forms that we now refer to as cusp forms and his conjectures formulated in this connection, and their later generalization, have come to play a more central role in the mathematics of today, serving as a kind of focus for the attention of quite a large group of the best mathematicians of our time. Other discoveries like the mock-theta functions are only in very early stages of being understood and no one can yet assess their real importance. So the final verdict is certainly not in, and it may not be in for a long time, but the estimates of Ramanujan's stature in mathematics certainly have been growing over the years. There is no doubt about that."

The prestigious Fields Medal, and its obverse, with its 1950 winner Atle Selberg (who shared the 1950 award with Laurent Schwartz of France).

Ramanujan's Notebooks

The history of the Notebooks, in brief, is the following: Ramanujan had noted down the results of his findings, without proofs, as in G.S. Carr's "A Synopsis of Elementary Results, a book on pure Mathematics", in three Notebooks, between the years 1903 – 1914, before he left for England.

These were the Notebooks which he showed to his benefactors to convince them about his abilities as a mathematician. The results in these Notebooks were organized by him.

The first Notebook has 16 Chapters in 134 Pages. The second Notebook contains 21 Chapters and is in 252 Pages. The third Notebook contains 33 pages of unorganized material, included at the end of Volume 2 of the facsimile edition, first published by the Tata Institute of Fundamental Research, Bombay, in 1957, and reprinted in the centenary year of his birth, 1987.

The first chapter of Notebook 1 is the only one which has a title "Magic Squares" and is 3 pages long. The first Chapter of Notebook 2 is on Magic squares but it is a longer chapter in 8 pages and has no title like all other chapters in both his Notebooks.

Note that Chapter 12, p.86, of Notebook 1 is on hypergeometric series, while Chapter 10, p.113, of Notebook 2 is also on the same subject of hypergeometric series. Both the chapters start with the most general summation theorem known in mathematics as the 7F6(1) summation theorem, or as Dougall – Ramanujan summation theorem.

This summation theorem, in modern day notation (invented by Barnes) is often referred to as the 7F6(1) summation theorem – a key formula in Chapter XII of Ramanujan's Notebook 1 (and Chapter X of Notebook 2) and has been completely edited by Hardy, who observed that Dougall published it in 1909 and Ramanujan had it in his Notebooks which have no dates. For this reason, he would refer to it as the Hardy-Ramanujan summation theorem (rather than as the Ramanujan-Hardy theorem). Furthermore, Hardy wrote:

"In algebra, Ramanujan's main work was concerned with hypergeometric series and continued fractions. (I use the word algebra, of course, in its old-fashioned sense). These subjects suited him exactly, and here he was unquestionably one of the greatest masters. These subjects suited him exactly, and here he was unquestionably one of the greatest masters. There are now three famous identities, the "Dougall-Ramanujan identity" … and the "Rogers-Ramanujan identities", in which he had been anticipated by British mathematicians …

"As regards hypergeometric series one may say, roughly, that he discovered the formal theory, set out in Bailey's tract, "Generalized Hypergeometric Series" (Cambridge Tracts in Mathematics and Mathematical Phyiscs, (Hafner Publishing Co., New York, 1964), as it was known up to 1920. There is something about it in Carr, and more in Chrystal's 'Algebra', and no doubt he got his start from that. …

"Ramanujan seems to have found the formula about 1910 or 1911, but he had been anticipated by Dougall. The formula looks formidable, but Dougall's proof is very simple. I imagine that Ramanujan argued similarly, but there is nothing in the notebooks to show." – these quotations are from p.12 and p.102 of Hardy's "Ramanujan: Twelve Lectures …".

Saalschütz's theorem (1890) for a terminating 3F2 (1) and Dixon's theorem (1903) for any convergent well-poised series of the 3F2 (a, b, c; 1+a-b, 1+a-c; 1), are two of the important results of Ramanujan obtained as limiting cases of this key formula, called by Hardy as the Dougall-Ramanujan summation theorem for a ('well-poised' hyper-geometric series, denoted as the) 7F6 (1). Ramanujan never published this result and it is found only in his Notebooks. Most of the results in these chapter XII of the first Notebook and chapter X of the second Notebook have been derived by Ramanujan from this key formula. Ramanujan had only access to Carr's Synopsis which contained the definition of the hypergeometric series and the Gauss summation theorem. This abridged Synopsis, published in 1886, did not contain the generalization of the Gauss hypergeometric series, 2F1 (z), by Clausen who, in 1828, introduced a series which is a generalization of Gauss's series with three numerator and two denominator parameters.

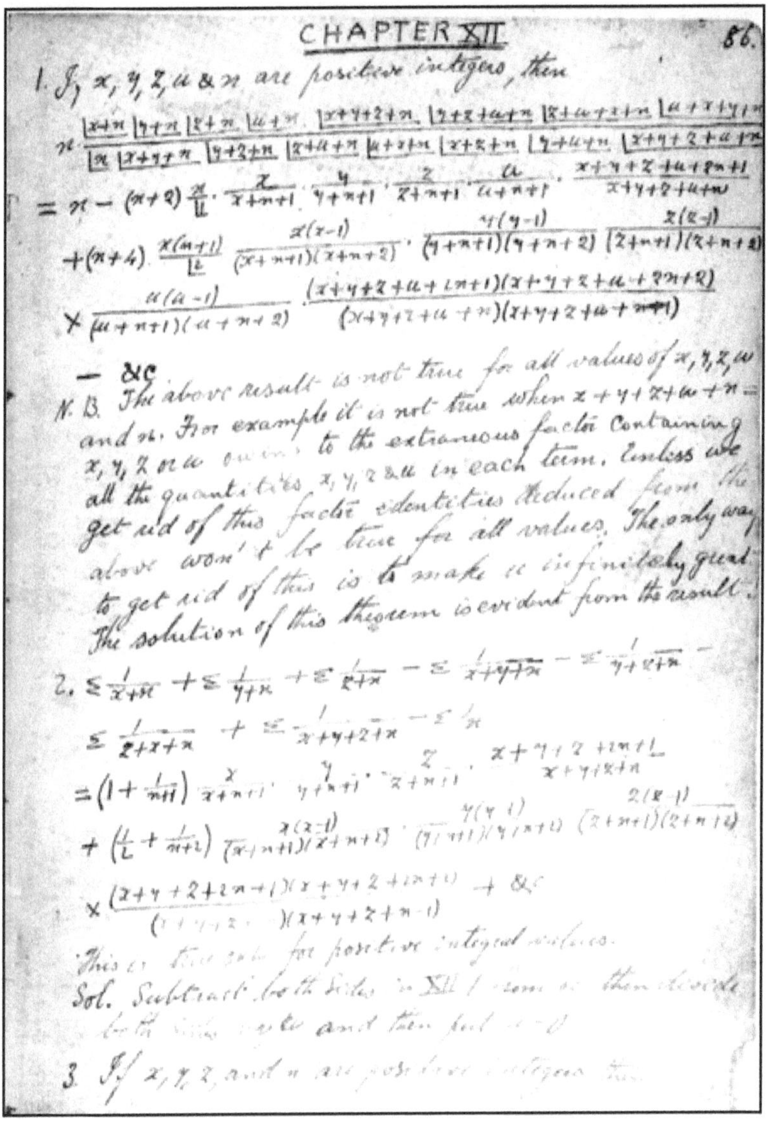

CHAPTER XII

(Facsimile of a handwritten manuscript page numbered 86. The page contains handwritten mathematical derivations — a summation theorem, expansions with factorial/Pochhammer expressions, an N.B. note, and numbered entries 2 and 3. The handwriting is only partly legible.)

1. If x, y, z, u & n are positive integers, then

$$n \cdot \frac{\lfloor x+n \ \lfloor y+n \ \lfloor z+n \ \lfloor u+n \ \lfloor x+y+z+n \ \lfloor y+z+u+n \ \lfloor z+u+y+n \ \lfloor u+x+y+n}{\lfloor x \ \lfloor x+y+n \ \lfloor y+z+n \ \lfloor z+u+n \ \lfloor u+x+n \ \lfloor x+z+n \ \lfloor y+u+n \ \lfloor x+y+z+u+n}$$

$$= n - (n+2)\,\frac{x}{\lfloor 1} \cdot \frac{x}{x+n+1} \cdot \frac{y}{y+n+1} \cdot \frac{z}{z+n+1} \cdot \frac{u}{u+n+1} \cdot \frac{x+y+z+u+2n+1}{x+y+z+u+n}$$

$$+ (n+4)\,\frac{x(x+1)}{\lfloor 2} \cdot \frac{x(x-1)}{(x+n+1)(x+n+2)} \cdot \frac{y(y-1)}{(y+n+1)(y+n+2)} \cdot \frac{z(z-1)}{(z+n+1)(z+n+2)}$$

$$\times \frac{u(u-1)}{(u+n+1)(u+n+2)} \cdot \frac{(x+y+z+u+2n+1)(x+y+z+u+2n+2)}{(x+y+z+u+n)(x+y+z+u+n+1)}$$

$$- \&c.$$

N.B. The above result is not true for all values of x, y, z, u and n. For example it is not true when $x+y+z+u+n =$ to the extraneous factor containing x, y, z or u occurs in each term. Unless we get rid of this factor, identities deduced from the above won't be true for all values. The only way to get rid of this is to make n infinitely great. The solution of this theorem is evident from the result.

2. $$\Sigma \frac{1}{x+n} + \Sigma \frac{1}{y+n} + \Sigma \frac{1}{z+n} - \Sigma \frac{1}{x+y+n} - \Sigma \frac{1}{y+z+n}$$

$$\Sigma \frac{1}{z+x+n} + \Sigma \frac{1}{x+y+z+n} - \Sigma \frac{1}{n}$$

$$= \left(1 + \frac{1}{n+1}\right) \frac{x}{x+n+1} \cdot \frac{y}{y+n+1} \cdot \frac{z}{z+n+1} \cdot \frac{x+y+z+2n+1}{x+y+z+n}$$

$$+ \left(\frac{1}{2} + \frac{1}{n+2}\right) \frac{x(x-1)}{(x+n+1)(x+n+2)} \cdot \frac{y(y-1)}{(y+n+1)(y+n+2)} \cdot \frac{z(z-1)}{(z+n+1)(z+n+2)}$$

$$\times \frac{(x+y+z+2n+1)(x+y+z+2n+2)}{(x+y+z+n)(x+y+z+n+1)} + \&c.$$

This is true only for positive integral values.

Sol. Subtract both sides in XII / some or then divide both sides ... and then put ...

3. If x, y, z and n are positive integers, ...

P.86 in the first Notebook of Ramanujan on Hypergeometric series.
Entry 1 is the summation theorem for a 7F6 (1) series.
The best understood class of functions are called the hypergeometric functions, and the series associated with it is the hypergeometric series.

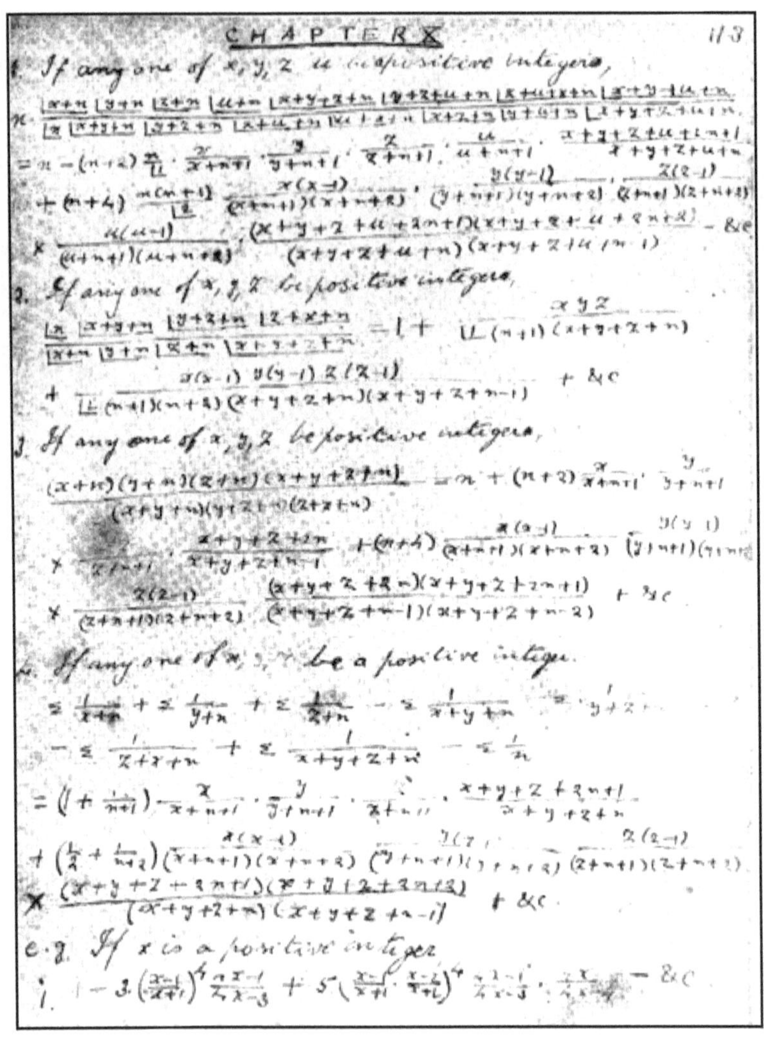

P.113 of Chapter X, Notebook 2 of Ramanujan. Notice that Entry 1 here is the same as Entry 1, P.86 of Chapter XII of his Notebook 1.

This lead to generalizations of the Gauss summation theorem (1812) for the 2F1(1), by Saalschutz (1880) for the 4F3 (1) , Dixon (1903) for the 3F2 (1), and Dougall - Ramanujan for the 7F6 (1). There are only 23 summation theorems in the whole of mathematics today.

Ramanujan communicated in his first letter to Hardy, in January 1913, four of his formulae from his Notebooks on hypergeometric series. After spending several months in 1923, three years after the death of Ramanujan, Hardy before giving up his work on the Entries of Ramanujan in his Notebooks wrote that Chapter XII of Ramanujan's Notebook "contains in a condensed form practically everything that is known about the summation and transformation of this series . . . It contains 47 theorems, many of them followed by a separate statement of a number of corollaries and particular cases. Thus, formula (40) is followed by 'examples' 1 − 18."

S.R. Ranganathan in his book, "Ramanujan: the Man and the Mathematician", (on p.57) recalls that, in March 1925, in a conversation Hardy said to him:

"This work has taken me several weeks. If I am to edit the entire notebook, it will take the whole of my life-time. I cannot do my own work. This would not be proper".

"As regards hypergeometric series one may say, roughly, that he discovered the formal theory, set out in Bailey's tract, "Generalized Hypergeometric Series" (Cambridge Tracts in Mathematics and Mathematical Phyiscs, (Hafner Publishing Co., New York, 1964), as it was known up to 1920. There is something about it in Carr, and more in Chrystal's 'Algebra', and no doubt he got his start from that. ... Ramanujan seems to have found the formula about 1910 or 1911, but he had been anticipated by Dougall. The formula looks formidable, but Dougall's proof is very simple. I imagine that Ramanujan argued similarly, but there is nothing in the notebooks to show."

− these quotations are from p.12 and p.102 of Hardy's "Ramanujan: Twelve Lectures ...". Saalschütz's theorem (1890) for a terminating 3F2 (1) and Dixon's theorem (1903) for any convergent well-poised series of the 3 F2 (a, b, c; 1+a-b, 1+a-c; 1), are two of the important results of Ramanujan obtained as limiting cases of his key formula, called by Hardy as the Dougall-Ramanujan summation theorem for a well-poised 7F6 (1).

Most of the results in that Chapter of Ramanujan can be derived from this key result. It is well - known that Ramanujan had access only to Carr's " Synopsis" in which there is only a definition of the Gauss summation theorem for the hyper-geometric 2F1 (a,b; c; 1) series.

It is Ramanujan's 'natural' genius and his mathematical vision which enabled him to construct for himself the most general summation theorem known in the mathematical world with just that hint.

In Chapters XII, XIII and XV of the first Notebook and Chapters X and XI of the second Notebook Ramanujan studied hypergeometric series. His Chapters X and XI of the second Notebook have, respectively, 35 and 36, numbered Entries on hypergeometric series, a proof for each one of which has been provided by Bruce C. Berndt in Part II of his five Part magnum opus entitled: "Ramanujan's Notebooks" – Part I (1985), Part II (1989), Part III (1991), Part IV (1994), and Part V (1997), Springer-Verlag, New York. Below find with Gauss's Portrait and the 'normal' or Gauss distribution on it.

It would be most appropriate for the Government of India to honour Ramanujan in a similar manner, in this 2012 Year of Mathematics, in India.

Carl Friedrich Gauss and the 10 Deutsch Mark Note of Germany with Gauss's Portrait and the 'normal' or Gauss distribution on it. It would be most appropriate for the Government of India to honour

Ramanujan in a similar manner, in this 2012 Year of Mathematics, in India.

Ramanujan wrote down the first few terms in each series and did not use any notation, like that due to E.W. Barnes (1907), for the hypergeometric series. So it was easy for him to discern the elegance in formulas involving series. In this context, Askey's article entitled: "Ramanujan and Hpergeometric and Basic Hyper-geometric Series", in the Proceedings of the Ramanujan International Symposium on Analysis, December 26 – 28 (1987), edited by N.K. Thankare, K.C. Sharma and T.T. Raghunathan, for Macmillan (India) Limited (1989), is a good starting point for the interested student who wants to learn about Ramanujan's pioneering contributions to ordinary and hypergeometric series. It is due to Ramanujan's discovery of all that was known in Europe about hypergeometric series without any knowledge about the same from published works of those times, which makes us compare Ramanujan to the versatile Gauss who wrote down the differential equation and published a seminal paper on the subject of hypergeometric series in 1812. Note: A year later, Kummer found 24 solutions for the Gauss 2nd order ordinary differential equation equation. The author wondered from the first time he came across the monographs of W.N. Bailey (1935) and his student Lucy J. Slater (1966) about these solutions written in a few pages of their monographs. Only in 2005 was it possible for him to construct a function of six variables, associated with the six sides of a cube, and show that by construction, a 2F1 (a , b; c; z) series, with Gauss's 1812 observation with foresight, that it should be considered as <u>a function of four variables</u> – and not as a function of the variable z, treating a, b as the numerator and c as the denominator parameters – led to a single equation on which superposing the 24 symmetries of the cube results in revealing the 24 solutions, a truly remarkable result. Ref: The finite group of Kummer solutions, S. Lievens, K. Srinivasa Rao and J. Vander Jeugt, in the journal Integral Transforms and Special Functions, vol. 16 (2005) pages 153 – 158.

Ramanujan obtained results on continued fraction from the three-term recurrence relation he derived for himself for the hypergeometric series. He rediscovered not only many of the classical results of Euler, Gauss and Heine and others on hypergeometric series and continued fractions but also discovered many new results. His 'Lost' Notebook contains many results related to Heine's q-series and some of the q-continued fractions are related to the modular functions. In the words of Professor K.G. Ramanathan of the Tata Institute of Fudamental Research, Bombay, at the time of the Birth Centenary of Ramanujan, in 1987: "The exploitation of this relationship between modular functions and continued fractions is one of the most beautiful aspects of Ramanujan's work of continued fractions".

The Tata Institute of Fundamental Research, Colaba, Bombay.

Prof. Dr. Homi Bhabha its Founder Director was instrumental in approaching the Prime Minister Nehru to bring out the facsimile edition of the Notebooks of Srinivsa Ramanujan.

Ramanujan and the Taxi cab number 1729

The following is an oft repeated famous anecdote due to Hardy (ref. p. 12 and p. 21 of Hardy's "Ramanujan: Twelve Lectures ..."):

"He [Ramanujan] could remember the idiosyncrasies of numbers in an almost uncanny way. It was Littlewood who said that every positive integer was one of Ramanujan's personal friends. I remember going to see him once when he was lying ill in Putney. I had ridden in taxi-cab number 1729, and remarked that the number seemed to me rather a dull one, and that I hoped that it was not an unfortunate omen. 'No', he replied, 'it is a very interesting number, it is the smallest number expressible as a sum of two cubes in two different ways'. I asked him, naturally, whether he could tell me the solution of the corresponding problem for the fourth powers; and he replied, after a moment's thought, that he knew no obvious example, and supposed that the first such number must be very large".

The simplest known solution of the Diophantine equation:

$$x^4 + y^4 = u^4 + v^4,$$

with x, y, u and v being integers, is Euler's:

$$59^4 + 158^4 = 133^4 + 134^4 = 635318657.$$

Euler gave a solution involving two parameters, but no 'general' solution is known. This anecdote reveals Ramanujan's remarkable feeling for numbers and his sharp memory which made him recall one entry out of several thousands he had made in his Notebook just like that and the fact that he had not recorded in his Notebook the observation he made about 1729 which came from him, that "it is the smallest number which can be expressed as the sum of two cubes in two different ways", only when Hardy made an innocuous statement regarding the taxi cab number. It also reveals that Ramanujan did not write down all that he knew about any mathematical result he had noted down in his Notebooks.

Though the number 1729 itself finds no explicit mention in the Notebooks of Ramanujan, the above mentioned Euler equation or its solution:

$$1^3 + 12^3 = 9^3 + 10^3$$

finds mention in three Questions to the Journal of Indian Mathematical Society, (in Collected Paper of Srinivasa Ramanujan, P. 331) and in two places in Ramanujan's Notebooks (Vol. 2, p. 266 and p.387).

Explicitly, these are:

- Question 441 (Journal of the IMS, vol. V, p. 39):

  Shew that

  $$(6a^2 - 4ab + 4b^2)^3 = (3a^2 + 5ab - 5b^2)^3 + (4a^2 - 4ab + 6b^2)^3 + (5a^2 - 5ab - 3 b^2)^3,$$

  and find other quadratic expressions satisfying similar relations.

  [Solution by S. Narayanan, in Journal of the IMS, vol. VI, p. 226.]

- Question 661 (Journal of the IMS, vol. VII, p. 119):

  Solve in integers

  $$x^3 + y^3 + z^3 = u^6,$$

  and deduce the following:

  $$6^3 - 5^3 - 3^3 = 2^6, \qquad 8^3 + 6^3 + 1^3 = 3^6,$$
  $$12^3 - 10^3 + 1^3 = \qquad 3^6, 46^3 - 37^3 - 3^3 = 6^6,$$
  $$174^3 + 133^3 - 45^3 = \qquad 2^6, 1188^3 - 509^3 - 3^3 = 34^6.$$

  [Solution by N.B. Mitra, in Journal of the IMS, vol. XIII, p. 15 – 17. Additional solution and remarks by N.B. Mitra, JIMS, vol. XIV, p. 73 – 77.]

- Question 681 (Journal of the IMS, vol. VII, p. 160):

  Solve in integers

  $$x^3 + y^3 + z^3 = 1,$$

  and deduce the following:

  $$6^3 + 8^3 = 9^3 - 1, \qquad 9^3 + 10^3 = 12^3 + 1,$$
  $$135^3 + 138^3 = 172^3 - 1, \qquad 791^3 + 812^3 = 1010^3 - 1,$$

$$1161^3 + 11468^3 = 14258^3 + 1, \quad 65601^3 + 67402^3 = 83802^3 + 1.$$

[Partial solution by N.B. Mitra, in Journal of the IMS, vol. XIII, p. 17. See also N.B. Mitra, JIMS, vol. XIV, p. 73 – 77 (76 – 77).]

- If p, q, r are quantities so taken that

$$p + 3a^2 = q + 3ab = r + 3b^2 = (a + b)^2$$

and m and n are any two quantities, then

$$n(mp+nq)^3+m(mq+nr)^3 = m(np+mq)^3+n(nq+mr)^3.$$

A particular case of the above theorem is:

$$(3a^2 + 5ab - 5b^2)^3 + (4a^2 - 4ab + 6b^2)^3 + (5a^2 - 5ab - 3 b^2)^3$$
$$= (5a^2 - 5ab - 3 b^2)^3,$$

(Journal of the IMS, vol.2, p. 266.)

- If $\alpha^2 + \alpha \beta + \beta^2 = 3 \lambda \gamma^2$, then

$$(\alpha + \lambda^2 \gamma)^3 + (\lambda \beta + \gamma)^3 = (\lambda \alpha + \gamma)^3 + (\beta + \lambda^2 \gamma)^3.$$

(Journal of the IMS, vol.2, p. 387.)

Note that in the above 4-parameter solution for the Euler's equation, it has been observed (P.K. Srinivasan and T. Dharmarajanm, in 'An Introduction to Creativity of Ramanujan – an Instructional Guide to Mathematics Teachers in High Schools, a publication of the Association of Mathematics Teachers of India, 1987, p.43) that for

$$\alpha = 3, \ \beta = 0, \ \lambda = 3, \text{ and } \gamma = 1,$$

we will get

$$12^3 + 1^3 = 10^3 + 9^3 = 1729.$$

The fact that Ramanujan could come out spontaneously with the statement that 1729 is the smallest number that can be expressed as the sum of two cubes in two different ways, something which was obvious to him and which he therefore did not jot down in his Notebooks, proves that every integer is a 'personal friend' of Ramanujan as remarked by Professor J.E. Littlewood.

Hardy's statement that two thirds of the work of Ramanujan in India, contained in his Notebooks, consisted of rediscoveries, is refuted by Bruce Berndt who states, after his extensive studies of the Notebooks over two decades, trying to give a proof for each one of the 3254 Entries in the Notebooks, that this estimate of Hardy is too high.

In the Introduction to 'Ramanujan's Notebooks', Part V, Berndt states:

"This volume, however, should not be regarded as the closing chapter on Ramanujan's notebooks. Instead, it is just the first milestone on our journey to understanding Ramanujan's ideas. . . . It is our fervent wish that these volumes will serve as spring-boards for further investigations by mathematicians intrigued by Ramanujan's remarkable ideas. . . .

"Ramanujan remarked that several of his series arose from alternative theories of elliptic functions. . . . The first of the three alternative theories is the most interesting and the most important, and we feel that a large body of work remains to be discovered here".

It should be pointed out that Hardy observed that whenever he asked for a proof of any result of Ramanujan, Ramanujan was able to provide him more than one proof instantaneously and some of them ingenious.

Though the number 1729, sometimes referred to as Ramanujan number, or as Hardy-Ramanujan number, itself finds no explicit mention in the Notebooks, while Euler's equation and / or its solution:

$$x^3 + y^3 = u^3 + v^3 \text{ and } 1^3 + 12^3 = 9^3 + 10^3$$

finds mention in Questions 441, 661 and 668 proposed by Ramanujan in the Journal of the Indian Mathematical Society and in two places on p. 226 and p.387, in his second Notebook. Explicitly, for instance, Ramanujan's Q.441 is: "Shew that

$$(6a^2 - 4ab + 4b^2)^3 = (3a^2 + 5ab - 5b^2)^3 + (4a^2 - 4ab + 6b^2)^3$$
$$+ (5a^2 - 5ab - 3b^2)^3$$

and find other quadratic expressions satisfying similar relations". The solution for this problem has been provided by S. Narayanan and can be found in the book of S.R. Ranganathan entitled: "Ramanujan: the Man and the Mathematician" (1967). Observe that the last equation is indeed a two parameter solution to the Diophantine equation:

$$x^3 + y^3 = u^3 + v^3.$$

Note that every student of mathematics who encounters the Pythagoras theorem:

$$x^2 + y^2 = z^2$$

can also be taught the fact that the integer solutions of this equation are called Pythagorean triples: (3,4,5) since, $3^2 + 4^2 = 5^2$. Two significant simple facts must be stressed:

One, that every multiple of (3,4,5), namely (3n,4n,5n) for n = 1,2, ... is a solution and thus, there are an infinite number of solutions and secondly, below 100, there are 16 Pythogorean triples. Explicitly, they are:

(3,4,5) (5,12,13) (8,15,17) (7,24,25) (20,21,29) (12,35,37)

(9,40,41) (28,45,53) (11,60,61) (16,63,65) (33,56,65) (48,55,73)

(13,84,85) (36,77,85) (39,80,89) (65,72,97).

The Pythogorean triple can be formed by taking any m and n, such that m > n and then the triple is:

$$(2mn, m^2 - n^2, m^2 + n^2).$$

Hardy's statement that two thirds of Ramanujan's work in India, contained in the Notebooks, consisted of rediscoveries of results which were already known, is refuted by Bruce C. Berndt, who states, after his extensive studies of all the Entries of Ramanujan in his Notebooks and his published papers, that Hardy's estimate is too high.

Berndt set for himself the goal "to prove each of Ramanujan's theorems" states in the Introduction to Part I, of his five part work on "Ramanujan's Notebooks", states that:

"This volume, however should not be regarded as the closing chapter on Ramanujan's notebooks. Instead, it is just the first milestone on our journey to understanding Ramanujan's ideas. … It is our fervent wish that these volumes will serve as springboards for further investigations by mathematicians intrigued by Ramanujan's remarkable ideas. … Ramanujan remarked that several of his series arose from alternative theories of elliptic functions … The first of the three alternative theories is the most interesting and the most important, and we feel that a large body of work remains to be discovered here".

Ramanujan's work on hypergeometric series, contained in chapters X and XI of his second Notebook was edited by Hardy, as stated earlier. In the concluding part V, Berndt examines the unorganized pages in all the three Notebooks of Ramanujan on continued fractions, alternative theories of elliptic functions, class invariants and singular modulii, explicit values of theta functions, modular equations, infinite series, approximations and asymptotic expansions, etc. Berndt points out that "very few claims in this volume pertain to Ramanujan's published papers and problems."

Many theorems communicated by Ramanujan to Hardy in his January 16 and February 27, 1913, letters are in Chapters 22 and 31, of Berndt's book and in all, $759 + 605 + 834 + 491 + 565 = 3254$ theorems / Entries have been studied in Part I to V, authored by Professor Bruce C. Berndt. Hardy rightly estimated that the Notebooks of Ramanujan contained approximately 3000 – 4000 statements of theorems and besides editing one chapter of Ramanujan's second Notebook, in 1923, he tried to get them all edited by G.N. Watson and B.M. Wilson. But this did not work out due to the untimely death of Wilson. The tireless efforts of the indefatigable Bruce C. Berndt were necessary and it took him 22 years, from 1974 till 1996, to provide a proof for each of the Ramanujan Entries and in the process benefited a score of students to get their Ph.D. degrees. For motivating the student of mathematics, this five part publication will provide a plethora of results for further studies.

It is no exaggeration to say that as long as people do mathematics the work of Ramanujan and the stupendous effort of Bruce Berndt in editing the Notebooks of Ramanujan will be appreciated, as a significant contribution to mathematics.

Ratan P. Agarwal belongs to the school of ordinary and basic hypergeometric series in India. He has authored a three volume work entitled: "Resonance of Ranmanujan's Mathematics", Volumes 1 to 3, (1996). The author was inducted into the Special Functions group by Prof. R.P. Agarwal and the Director of the Institute of Mathematical Sciences, Professor E.C.G. Sudarshan encouraged and enabled the author to conduct a Workshop on Special Functions and Differential Equations (January 13 - 24, 1997), an International conference on Special Functions and their applications (September 23 – 27, 2002), at the Institute of Mathematical Sciences.

March 1919 Passport photograph

Ramanujan in Cambridge (1914 to 1919)

Graduation February 1918

CHAPTER 8

Chandrasekhar on Ramanujan

Dr. S. Chandrasekhar, on every one of his visits to India, ever since July 1936, when he first met Janaki Ramanujan, acquired the passport photograph of Ramanujan for Hardy, he made it a point to call on the lady. However, Chandrasekhar was seldom willing to talk about Ramanujan or his work on any occasion. In 1987, on the occasion of the birth centenary celebrations of Ramanujan, at the International Conference organized at Madras, he was requested to give the first lecture. Surprisingly, he chose to speak on Newton's Principia! Newton's Principia was the topic of study for Chandra during the last decade of his life. This is because Chandrasekhar had earlier spoken 'On Ramanujan' at the Banquet on June 3,1987, at an International conference organized at the University of Illinois, Urbana-Champagne, which we reproduce below:

Dr. S. Chandrasekhar, won the Nobel Prize for Physics, in 1983.

Alfred Nobel on The Nobel Prize

"On Ramanujan": S. Chandrasekhar

"I cannot clearly say anything that will relate to Ramanujan as a Mathematician, particularly in this company which includes among others, Professors Richard Askey, Bruce Benrdt, and George Andrews, who have devoted years to exploring and following his many trails. But I do share with Ramanujan the same cultural background in our early formative years: both of us originate in a common social background – he from Kumbakonam and I from Tanjore, both ancient centers of Tamil culture and not very for apart. Besides, Ramanujan's parents and my own grandparents lived in very similar social and financial circumstances. On this account I can probably visualize Ramanujan's background better than ever younger Indian colleagues of later generations.

"With this common background, I can perhaps throw some light on some conflicting statements that have been made about Ramanujan and 'God' by some of his Indian contemporaries. I refer here particularly to the colourful stories concerning Ramanujan's devotion to the Namakkal Goddess.

"Quite generally, it may be stated that among those who were brought up in south India during the first two decades of this century, there was (and probably still is) very little correlation between observance and belief. In particular, I can vouch from my own personal experience that some of the 'observations' that one followed were largely for the purposes of not offending the sensibilities of one's parents, relations, and friends.

"I can say a good deal on these matters, but I shall only state that I do not accept what has commonly been said and written about Ramanujan's religious beliefs.

"I corresponded with Hardy on this matter while he was preparing for his Harvard Lectures; and I was personally much more inclined to accept his view as expressed in a letter to me dated February 19, 1936. '… And my own view is that, at bottom and to a first approximation, R was (intellectually) as sound as infidel as Bertrand Russel or Littlewood. … One thing I am sure. R was not in the least the 'inspired idiot' that some people seem to have thought him. On the contrary, he was (except for a period when is mental equilibrium was definitely upset by illness) a very shrewd and sensible person: very individual, of course, and with a reasonable allowance of the minor eccentricities of genius, but fundamentally normal and sane.'

"And this view of Hardy's is corroborated by K. Anand Rao, himself a mathematician of distinction, who had been Hardy's student and Ramanujan's contemporary in Cambridge. Ananda Rao is well known and remembered for his contributions to the theory of Tauberian theorems, function-theory and the theory of Dirichlet series. He has written: 'In his nature he was simple, entirely free from affectation, with no trace whatever of his being self-conscious of his abilities. He was quite sociable, very polite and considerate to others. He was a man full of humour and a good conversationalist, and it was alwaus interesting to listen to him. On occasions when I met him, we used tot talk in homely Tamil. He could talk on many things besides mathematics …

"This view of Ananda Rao is not surprisingly the same as Hardy's as Hardy's . He has written, … 'the picture which I want to present to you is that of a man who had his peculiarities like other distinguished men, but a man in whose society one could take pleasure with whom one could drink tea discuss politics or mathematics.'

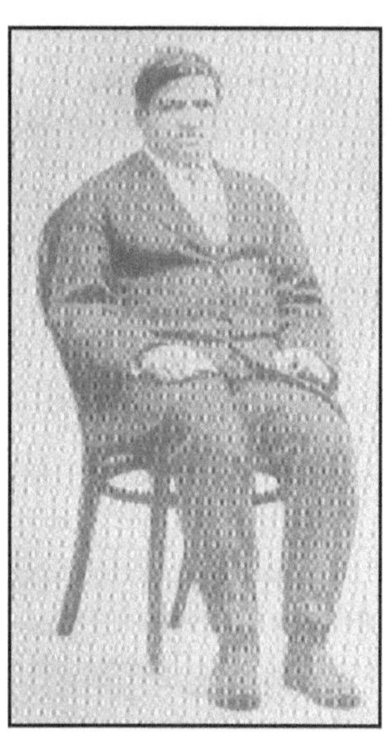

Ramanujan with his friends in Cambridge, 1918.
Standing: K. Ananda Rao, S.S. Suryanarayana Sastri, Tenneti Suryanarayana.
Seated: Srinivasa Ramanujan and T. Adinaryana Chetty.
Biographical details about these friends of Ramanujan are in
"Ramanujan: Essays and Surveys",
Edited by Bruce C. Berndt and Robert A. Rankin, AMS – LMS (2000).

"Let me now turn to the role of Ramanujan in the development of science in India during the early years of this century. Perhaps the best way I can give you a feeling for what Ramanujan meant to the young man going to schools and colleagues during the period 1915 – 1930 is to recall for you the way in which I first learned of Ramnanujan's name.

"It must have been a day in April 1920, when I was not quite ten years old, when my mother told me of an item in the newspaper of the day that a famous Indian mathematician, Ramanujan by name, had died the preceding day; and she told me further that Ramanujan had gone to England some years earlier, had collaborated with some famous English mathematicians, and that he had returned only very recently, and was well known internationally for what he had achieved. Though I had no idea at that time of what kind of a mathematician Ramanujan was, or indeed what scientific achievement meant, I can still recall the circumstances similar to my own, could have achieved what I could not grasp. I am sure that others were equally gladdened. I hope that it is not hard for you to imagine what the example of Ramanujan could have provided for young men and women of those times., beginning to look at the world with increasingly different perceptions.

"The fact that Ramanujan's early years were spent in a scientifically sterile atmosphere, that his life in India was not without hardships, that under circumstances at hat appeared to most Indians as nothing short of miraculous, he had gone to Cambridge, supported by eminent mathematicians, and had returned to India with every assurance that he would be considered in time, as one of the most original mathematicians of the century – these facts ere enough – more than enough – for aspiring young Indian students to break their bonds of intellectual confinement and perhaps soar the way that Ramanujan had.

"It may be argued, perhaps with some justice, that this was a sentimental attitude: Ramanujan represents so extreme a fluctuation from the norm that his being born an Indian must be considered to a large extent as accidental. But to the Indians of the time, Ramanujan was not unique in the way we think of him today. He was one of others who had, during that same period, achieved, in their judgement, comparably in science and in other areas of human activity. Gandhi, Motilal and Jawaharlal Nehru, Rabindranath Tagore, J.C. Bose, C.V. Raman, M.N. Saha, S.N. Bose, and a host of others, were in the forefront of the fermenting Indian scene. The twenties and the thirties were a period when young Indians were inspired for achievement and accomplishment b7 these men who they saw among them.

"I do not wish to leave the impression that Ramanujan's influence was only in this very generalized sense. I think it is fair to say that almost all the mathematicians who reached distinction during the three or four decades following Ramanujan were directly or indirectly inspired by his example.

"But Ramanujan's name inspired not only ambitious young men planning scientific careers; it also stimulated to action those with public concern. Let me give one example.

"When I was a student in Madras one of my classmates (who came from a very wealthy family) was one Alagappa Chettiar. We became friends; but our lives diverged along different paths after 1930. In the years before and during the second world war, Alagappa Chettiar prospered as an entrepreneur and became a noted philanthropist. He was in fact knighted by the British Government.

"During the late forties after the war, Sir Alagappa Chettiar (as he was then) wrote to me inquiring if it might be useful for him to found a mathematical institute in Madras named after Ramanujan. I enthusiastically supported the idea; and when I returned to India briefly in 1951, the Ramanujan Institute had been founded a few months earlier. Its first Director, T. Vijayaraghavan, was one of the most talented among Hardy's former students; he died at a comparatively early age in 1956. C.T. Rajagopal, a student of Ananda Rao, took over the Directorship from him. Already at that time the financial state of the Institute seemed shaky, since Alagappa Chettiar's fortune melted awa

Alagappa Chettiar

A view of the Ramanujan Institute for Advanced Study in Mathematics, University of Madras, Chepauk, Chennai – 600005.

housed in its own building opposite the Chepauk Cricket Grounds since 1972, on the Wallajah Road, very close to the famous Marina Beach. Robert Kanigel in his book: "The Man Who Knew Infinity: a life of the "In April 1957, when Alagappa Chettiar died, the fate of the Institute hung in the balance: Rajagopal wrote to me that the Institute 'will cease to exist on the first of next month,' whereupon I wrote to the Prime Minister (Jawaharlal Nehru), explaining the origin of the Institute and the seriousness of its condition. Nehru's prompt answer was refreshing: 'Even if you had not put in your strong recommendation in favour of the Ramanujan Institute of Mathematics, I would not have liked anything to happen which put an end to it. Now that you have also written to me on the subject, I shall keep in touch with this matter and I think I can assure you that the Institute will be carried on'. And it was; but haltingly and precariously for the next twelve years. It is at this Institute in Madras that Ramanujan's centennial will be celebrated by an International Conference in December.

"There is very little more I can say. My own view, sixty-six years after my first knowing of his name, is that India and the Indian scientific community were exceptionally fortunate in having before them the example of Ramanujan. It is hopeless to try to emulate him. But he was there even as the Everest is there."

The Ramanujan Institute, founded by Alagappa Chettiar, in 1951, was fused along with the Department of Mathematics of the University into a Center for Advanced Study in Mathematics and is permanently Mathematical Genius Ramanujan"(Scribner's 1991) wrote on this Ramanujan Institute: " ... it does not specialize in areas of mathematics

Ramanujan pursued, nor does its name bear anything like the luster of its namesake". This ought to make the Indian mathematical fraternity to sit up, having left it to George E. Andrews, Richard

Askey, Bruce C. Berndt, and a few other Ramanujan followers to make Ramanujan and his mathematics vibrant with life amongst the students in schools, colleges, universities and institutes in India. Attempts to get the name of the street on which the Ramanujan Institute for Advanced Study in Mathematics (RIASM) renamed after Ramanujan from its present Wallajah Road, have been unsuccessful, so far, till date.

Ramanujan's Passport Photograph

The Passport photograph of Ramanujan which has been considered as the most authentic one was first published in Hardy's "Ramanujan: Twelve Lectures on subjects suggested by his life and work", was taken when Ramanujan showed signs of improvement in his health after prolonged treatment for nearly 2 and ½ years at Nursing Homes and Sanatoria, since it was suspected that he had Tuberculosis (which was a dreaded contagious disease in those times), in 1919. It was necessitated by the fact, the British Government which did not ask him to get a Passport when he left Kumbakonam to go to Cambridge in March 1914, insisted on the Indian having a Passport to go back to his own country, India. We must thank them for this 'logical' situation, as in later years many stated that it was the only authentic photograph of Ramanujan and that we must be thankful to the British for that. However, there are other photographs also of Ramanujan, in the Journal of the Indian Mathematical Society's issues: one in which his Fellowship of the Royal Society is announced in 1918; and the one in which tributes have been paid to him on his demise in 1920.

However, we reproduce below the two letters of Dr. Chandrasekhar wrote to Hardy on the passport Photograph of Ramanujan, on August 4 and December 28, 1937, respectively:

The University of Chicago

Yerkes Observatory
WILLIAMS BAY WIS
1937 August 4

Dear Hardy,

I remember your telling me that when Ramanujan's collected papers were being edited, it was your original intention to include a portrait of R., but eventually you had to abandon the plan as no good photograph was available.

So, when I was in India last summer, I made an effort to find a reasonably good photograph. I met Mrs. Ramanujan – his wife, who incidentally is having a rather difficult life, some of her unscrupulous relatives having swindled her out of such financial resources as R. had left her – and it transpired that the only photograph of R (other than the one where he is "cap and gown") available in his passport photograph taken prior to his leaving England.

I had a negative taken of his passport photograph (which is now in my possession) and had an enlargement professionally made. I am sending you by separate cover an enlarged photograph of R, and as you will see it is a reasonably good one. I am not in a position to judge how 'true' it is, but I have it on Mrs. Ramanujan's authority that the rather worried look R has in the picture was extremely frequented during his last year.

I do not know if you would want to include this photograph in your book on R – I refer to your Harvard lectures and I do not know either if the enclosed enlargement would be good enough for reproduction purposes. In any case I think a good professional must be able to use the original negative I have and if it should be needed, I shall be only too glad to loan it. I have some more spare copies of the enlargements of R and if you should know others who may like to have a copy of R's photograph perhaps you could ask them to write to me.

With kindest regards,
Yours sincerely,
Chandrasekhar.

<u>P.S.</u> In any case, I should be glad to know what you think of the photograph.

Dr. S. Chandrasekhar with   *K.C. Wali's 'Chandra'*   *Chandra receiving the*
King of Sweden receiving the   *a Biography*   *medal from President*
Nobel Prize for Physics (1983)   *Lyndon B. Johnson.*

Some of the copies of the photograph referred to in this letter of Chandra to Hardy are still in the collection of papers of Ramanujan at the Wren Library of the Trinity College, Cambridge.

The University of Chicago

Yerkes Observatory
WILLIAMS BAY WIS
1937 August 28

Dear Hardy,

Many thanks for your letter of Dec. 15. I am very glad to learn of your intention to include the photograph in your book.

I am enclosing the negative from which the enlargement I sent you was made. Also a rather good copy of the same size as the negative and four rather poor copies of the enlargement. I am afraid that my own efforts at copying from the enlargement proved less successful than I had hoped! I am however certain that a professional photographer can make even better enlargements from the negative than the one I sent you.

My impression is that the college has no portrait of R. in its collection of fellows – perhaps you would be so kind as to pass on one of the four copies I am sending.

With the seasons greetings and with kind regards,

Yours very sincerely,
S. Chandrasekhar.

Jawaharlal Nehru, the first Prime Minister of Independent India, reputed for his book, "Discovery of India", was genuinely interested in Science and Technology. We have already seen that Chandrasekhar appealed to him for the continuance of the Ramanujan Institute. The letter of Chandrasekhar appealed to him for the continuance of the Ramanujan Institute. The letter of Chandrasekhar to Nehru and the latter's reply are preserved in the Nehru Memorial Museum.

We reproduce here the reference to Ramanujan contained in Nehru's 'Discovery of India':

"Mathematics in India inevitably makes one think of one extraordinary figure of recent times. This was Srinivasa Ramanujam. Born in a poor Brahmin family in South India, having no opportunities for a proper education, he became a clerk in the Madras Port Trust. But he was bubbling over with some irrepressible quality of instinctive genius and played about with numbers and equations in his spare time. By a lucky chance he attracted the attention of a mathematician who sent some of his amateur work to Cambridge in England. People there were impressed and a scholarship was arranged for him. So he left his clerk's job and went to Cambridge and during a very brief period there did work of profound value and amazing originality. The Royal Society of England went rather out of their way and made him a Fellow, but he died two years later, probably because of tuberculosis, at the age of 33. Professor Julian Huxley has, I believe, referred to him somewhere as the greatest mathematicians of the century.

"Ramanujan's brief life and death are symbolic of conditions in India. Of our millions how few get any education at all, how many live on the verge of starvation; of even those who get some education and have nothing to look forward to but a clerkship in some office on a pay that is usually far less than the unemployment dole in England. If life opened its gates to them and offered them food and healthy conditions of living and education and opportunities of growth, how many among these millions would be eminent scientists, educationsts, technicians, industrialists, writers and artists, helping to build a new India and new world ?"

Q. 289 (Jour. I M S IV, p.226) :

Find the values of :

(i) $\sqrt{1+2\sqrt{1+3\sqrt{1+4\sqrt{1+5\sqrt{1+\bullet\bullet\bullet}}}}}$

(ii) $\sqrt{6+2\sqrt{7+3\sqrt{8+4\sqrt{9+5\sqrt{10+\bullet\bullet\bullet}}}}}$

Ramanujan's solution for Q. 289 (i) :

$$f(n) = n(n+2) = n\sqrt{(n+2)^2}$$
$$= n\sqrt{n^2+4n+4}$$
$$= n\sqrt{1+(n+1)(n+3)}$$
$$= n\sqrt{1+f(n+1)}$$
$$= n\sqrt{1+(n+1)\sqrt{1+f(n+2)}}$$
$$= n\sqrt{1+(n+1)\sqrt{1+(n+2)\sqrt{1+\bullet\bullet\bullet}}}$$

For $n=1$,
$$3 = \sqrt{1+2\sqrt{1+3\sqrt{1+4\sqrt{1+\bullet\bullet\bullet}}}}$$

Ramanujan's solution for Q. 289 (ii) :

$$f(n) = n(n+3) = n\sqrt{(n+3)^2}$$
$$= n\sqrt{n^2+6n+9}$$
$$= n\sqrt{(n+5)+(n+1)(n+4)}$$
$$= n\sqrt{(n+5)+f(n+1)}$$
$$= n\sqrt{(n+5)+(n+1)\sqrt{(n+6)+f(n+2)}},$$

$$n(n+3) = n\sqrt{(n+5)+(n+1)\sqrt{(n+6)+(n+2)\sqrt{(n+7)+\bullet\bullet\bullet}}}$$

For $n=1$,
$$4 = \sqrt{6+2\sqrt{7+3\sqrt{8+4\sqrt{9+\bullet\bullet\bullet}}}}$$

The Q.289 and its solutions also appeared in JIMS. But the result in his Notebook 2, as an entry shows their generalization (with three integer parameters x, n and a)!

Entry 4, Notebook 2 :

$$x+n+a = n\sqrt{ax+(n+a)^2+x\sqrt{a(x+n)+(n+a)^2+(x+n)\sqrt{\&c}}}$$

e. g . i. $3 = 1\sqrt{1+2\sqrt{1+3\sqrt{1+4\sqrt{1+\&c}}}}$ ($x=2$, $n=1$, $a=0$)

ii. $4 = 1\sqrt{6+2\sqrt{7+3\sqrt{8+4\sqrt{9+\&c}}}}$. ($x=2$, $n=1$, $a=1$)

Chapter 9

A remarkable story

The Srinivasa Ramanujan Medal of the Indian National Science Academy was conferred on Dr. S. Chandrasekhar, in 1968. So, that year, Chandra came to India and gave the Nehru Memorial Lecture and the Ramanujan Lecture. Besides he had a meeting with Mrs. Janaki Ramanujan. What happened on that occasion is recorded to us in the chapter of 'Conversations with Chandra' by Kameshwar C. Wali in his book: 'Chandra', The University Chicago Press, Chicago (1991) and also Penguin Books India, New Delhi (1990), and it is reproduced below:

"I leanred of the incident from a conversation I had with Hardy at dinner in Trinity during the spring of 1936. Hardy arrived a little late but bandaged, and he sat at the table opposite me. The fact that he was bandaged naturally aroused the concern of those around him, and when questioned, he told a remarkable story. It's rather elaborate. You may want to reproduce it from the talk I gave to a private club at the University of Chicago.

The following is from S. Chandrasekhar, Notes and Records of the Royal Society, vol. 30 (1976), p. 249 and this account is now in print in 'Littlewood's Miscellany', Edited by Bela Bollobas, London University Press (1986). Also, the Madras city based newspaper 'The Hindu' carried the story, on November 17, 1968, under the heading:

When U.K. Policemen winked at an offence.

"It appeared that he [Hardy] was in London during the day and while crossing Piccadilly Circus a motorcycle hit him and dragged him along. He was bruised but only superficially. Nevertheless,

Hardy was escorted to the Scotland Yard by the policeman who had arrested the cyclist in order that Hardy could report what had happened. After Hardy had given the appropriate evidence and was about to leave, a messenger came to him and told him that a senior officer of the Scotland Yard wanted to see him. Hardy was slightly surprised. But the officer treated him with great courtesy, asked him to be seated and said, "Professor Hardy, I have been wanting to see you for many years. In fact, I have waited for this occasion for seventeen years. Do you know that we have had evidence in our files here to arrest you for giving false evidence?" Hardy was a little surprised and the officer continued. "Do you remember, Professor Hardy, that in February 1918, an Indian mathematician had tried to commit suicide by falling before the train in an underground tube station ?" His intention was thwarted and he was arrested and brought to Scotland Yard. I was in charge of that case. And you arrived later to give evidence". At this point I should digress, even as Hardy did while narrating his encounter with the officer of the Scotland Yard.

"Ramanujan had been quite ill during the winger of 1917 and apparently ina astate of extreme depression. Ramanujan in fact had tried to commit suiceide in the manner described by the officer; but by a series of miracles (like the switch being turned off by a guardsman, and the train coming to a stop just a few feet ahead of where Ramanujan had fallen) he had saved. To con tinue with the story.

"When you arrived at Scotland Yard, Professor Hardy, you told us that Ramanujan was a Fellow of the Royal Society and as such could not be arrested. We released Ramanujan and you left apparently believing that you had bluffed us; but in fact you had not. You knew as well as we did that Fellow of the Royal Society are not immune from arrest. But you also told a lie. At the time of this incident Ramanujan was not in fact a Fellow of the Royal Society. But you knew that he would be elected a month later but that is not the same thing. Nevertheless, on inquiry we found that the man whom we had arrested was indeed reputed to be a great mathematician and we in Scotland Yard did not want to spoil that lie. And so we let you believe that you had convinced us. But I have always hoped that an occasion would arise when I could tell you that we knew all along that you were telling a falsehood had perjured yourself. The occasion has now come; but I am not going to arrest you".

"I cannot quite recall whether it was on this same occasion, or on a later occasion, that Littlewood referred to Ramanujan's attempt to commit suicide in connection with his (Ramanujan's) election to a Fellowship at Trinity. There is apparently a rule that one who is medically insane cannot be elected to a Fellowship at Trinity. And Littlewood (who was one of the electors during the year that Ramanujan was a candidate) was afraid that Ramanujan's "insanity" in having attempted suicide might be brought up to disqualify his election; and on that account Littlewood said that he had gone to the electors meeting with a medical certificate to the effect that Ramanujan was not afflicted by insanity. And Littlewood added that he was extremely glad that no occasion arose which required him to produce the certificate.

[Our conversation continues.]

"You know there is a sequel to that story. In 1968 I gave the Nehru Memorial Lecture and the Ramanujan Lecture at the Indian National Academy of Sciences. They now call it the Indian National Science Academy. And, since it was the Ramanujan Memorial Lecture, I told the stories which Hardy and Littlewood had told me about Ramanujan's election to Trinity Fellowship and the Fellowship of the Royal Society. In that context, I mentioned Ramanujan'a attempted suicide. But it appeared in the newspaper the following day with big headlines, "Ramanujan tried to commit suicide", and told the story in a garbled way. I was astonished at the opposition it created. Everybody though I was ill-advised in telling that story. I went to Bangalore to see Raman, and one of the first things he said was, "Why do you want to defame that man?" Then there was a letter in the Times of India saying that my motive in recounting the incident was to enhance my own personal reputation at the expense of Ramanujan's. I was very depressed by that reaction. A few days later when I went to Madras, I was met at the library by a young man who introduced himself as a neighbor of Mrs. Ramanujan; and he told me that Mrs. Ramanujan was anxious to see me. I was naturally worried that she would be very upset about it. However, she told me that my account of Ramanujan's attempted suicide had cleared up certain things about her life, which was so tragic. I have written up things she told me in the Royal Society notes, but not for the public, because I don't know whether it is the kind of thing one should write without giving proper account of the whole story. Just one remark, Mrs. Ramanujan told me, for instance, that Ramanujan's mother put every kind of obstacle in their married life. …

"It is known (recorded, for example, by Hardy) that during Ramanujan's years in England, he received very few letters from his family in India. And Hardy attributed Ramanujan's depression during his later years in Cambridge to his 'misunderstandings' with his family. Ramanujan used to write regularly to his wife, but apparently did not pass them on. Ramanujan's wife could not write to him because she did not have the money for postage. …

"It throws an entirely different light. Yet he made some of his great contributions to mathematics during his four years in England. So I did write of my visit with Mrs. Ramanujan and sent it to the Royal Society Archives in London with his photograph and other things. They asked me whether they should publish it in their notes and records. I have not given them permission, but I have a feeling that it should be published sometime."

Professors Bruce C. Berndt and Robert A. Rankin did look into these Notes left behind by Chandra, before they completed their book: "Ramanujan: Letters and Commentary" and in a private communication from Professor Berndt, we learn that these Notes are only details of what we already know.

The 'Lost' Notebook of Ramanujan

After Ramanujan returned to India, though he was seriously ill and bed ridden with suspected tuberculosis and obtained the best medical attention possible, he was working at a furious pace, continuously, as recounted to several visitors by his wife Janakiammal, that his life-long habit was to work on a slate with a slate-pencil and transfer the final results to a Notebook or sheets of paper and that "a vast quantity of papers containing Ramanujan's notes were handed over to the University after his death". Three days after Ramanujan died, his brother S. Lakshminarasimhan, in a letter to Hardy, dated April 29, 1920, informing him about his demise, wrote: "All his MSS that were in his trunk were handed over on the day of his death to Mr. Ramachandra Row's son in law, since the former is at Nilgiris. Not only those but also the journals, magazines – all he possessed except the books which he had, were taken away by them".

George Eyre Andrews.

The 'lost' Notebook.

In a letter to Hardy, dated 3 December 1920, Ramachandra Rao, wrote: "Ramanujan's M.S.S., whatever they are, are with me and will be handed over intact to the University of Madras who I understand is already in correspondence with you regarding the methods of publication".

These papers reached Hardy, who should have passed them on to G.N. Watson and hence to their final destination – viz. the estate of Professor Watson, in the underground cellar of Trinity College – after he wrote several papers inspired by Ramanujan's results, until their discovery in 1976 by Professor George E. Andrews. Professor Watson died in February 1965 and a decade later in the spring of 1976, when Professor George E. Andrews of the Pennsylvania State University was going through the estate of Watson, he discovered a box of papers:

"The most interesting item in this box was a manuscript of more than one hundred pages in Ramanujan's distinctive handwriting which contains over six hundred mathematical formulae listed one after the other without proof. It is my contention that this manuscript, or notebook, was written during the last year of Ramanujan's life after his return to India from England. My evidence for this assertion is all indirect; in the words of Stephen Leacock, 'It is what we call circumstantial evidence – the same that people are hanged for' ".

Ramanujan died on April 26, 1920 at 10 A.M. and his death was mourned by the elite of Madras and all over the country, as he was by then a celebrity, who rose from Failed F.A. of Madras University to B.A. of Cambridge and a Fellow of the Royal Society, London – a meteoric rise from Kumbakonam to Cambridge! When the news the sudden demise reached Hardy through a letter from Madras, Hardy was surprised and shocked, since Ramanujan even in his only letter to Hardy, written in January 1920, did not mention about his ailment but only wrote about his discovery of the 'mock' theta functions and opening up yet another new vista for research. Thus, the death of Ramanujan after a brief life span of 32 years 4 months and 4 days came as a great shock to Hardy, who had arranged for a Trinity College Fellowship of £250 for six years sanctioned for Ramanujan when he was to return from India for further researches. It is to the eternal credit of the University of Madras and the then Governor of Madras, Lord Pentland, the ex-officio Chancellor of the University that all the financial sanctions – the first ever Fellowship for research in mathematics, the funds for his visit and stay at Cambridge from 1914 – 1919, the supplementary support for his passage by ship to and fro and initial outfit, and the continued support to Ramanujan after his return and the award of a pension to his widow after his return. This clearly is an indication of the whole-hearted support of the authorities in India to nurture the talent of the mathematical genius Ramanujan. The first recognition of his precocious nature was by his adoring mother, a staunch devotee of Namagirithayar of Namakkal.

His mentor was S. Narayana Iyer, could garner the support of influential people like Dewan Bahadur Ramachandra Rao, V. Ramaswamy Iyer and P.V. Seshu Iyer, through whose orchestrated effort the Registrar and the Chancellor of the University of Madras, ex-officio the Governor of Madars presidency, Lord Pentland, rose to the occasion to bring Ramanujan into contact with Professor Hardy and the rest is history! Surprisingly, while the name of the Registrar, Dewsbury, finds a mention everywhere in the story of Ramanujan, the Vice Chancellor's name does not find a mention anywhere and he was P.S. Sivaswamy Iyer. He was the Vice Chancellor of the University of Madras during 1916 – 1918. His brother Dr. P.S. Chandrasekhara Iyer, M.D., after his return from England, was the specialist who was invited to Kumbakonam to examine the ailing Ramanujan with the hope he would be able to diagnose the cause for the sickness and provide him medical relief. With hindsight we now know that despite the best medical attention that was provided to Ramanujan, the diagnosis was a confirmation of the British finding of Tuberculosis (which was questioned and proved not correct by Professor Rankin and Dr. Young, who concluded that he died of untreated hepatic amoebiasis).

Three others who did play smaller but significant roles in the life Ramanujan are to be mentioned. They are Professor E.W. Middlemast, Mathematics Professor at Engineering College in

Madras, Professor E.H. Neville who came on a visit to give lectures on Complex Analysis to the Mathematics Honours students of the University of Madras and Professor G.T. Walker, the Director General of Meteorological Observatories from Simla, who came on an official visit to the meteorological center in Madras.

Quotations of Ramanujan and about Ramanujan

- "An equation for me has no meaning, unless it expresses a thought of God".

- The quantity $2^n - 1$ [for Ramanujan] stood for "the primordial God and several identities:

  When n is 0, the expression denotes zero, there is Nothing;
  when n is 1, the expression denotes unity, the Infinite God;
  when n is 2, the expression denoted Trinity;
  when n is 3, the expression denotes 7, the Saptha Rsihis, and so on ."

- "If I die, please hand these [Notebooks] ove to Professor Singaravelu Mudaliar [of Pachaiyappa's College] or to the British Profess, Edward B. Ross, of the Madras Christian College."

- "I have [very rarely] encountered a pupil who could face the simplest problem involving the ideas of infinity, limit, or continuity with a vestige of the confidence which he could deal with questions of far greater intrinsic difficulty'. – G.H. Hardy.

- Years later he [Hardy] contrived an informal scale of natural mathematical ability on which he gave himself a 25 and Littlewood a 30. To David Hilbert, the most eminent mathematician of his day, he assigned an 80. To Ramanujan he gave 100. – Robert Kanigel, in "The Man Who Knew Infinity".

G.T. Walker

E.W. Middlemast

E.H. Neville

- G.H. Hardy sought for his friend the Fellowship of the Royal Society, London and for this he detailed Ramanujan's "Qualification" in his distinctive calligraphic hand: "Distinguished as a pure mathematician, particularly for his investigations in elliptic functions and the theory of numbers".

- "Elegance, depth and surprise, are beautifully intertwined" [in the work of Ramanujan on partitions].

- "It is perhaps useless to speculate as to his history had he been introduced to modern ideas and methods at sixteen instead of twenty-six. It is not extravagant to suppose that he might have become the greatest mathematician of his time", wrote Hardy soon after the death of Ramanujan and that Ramanujan laboured under "an impossible handicap, a poor solitary Hindu pitting his brains against the accumulated wisdom of Europe".

- Of 104 candidates nominated for the Fellowship of the Royal Society of London (F.R.S.), Ramanujan was one of 15 selected in February 1918 and the citation for the Award read "Srinivasa Ramanujan, Trinity College, Cambridge. Research student in Mathematics, ddistinguihsed as a pure mathematician particularly for his investigations in elliptic functions and the theory of numbers".

- "In his nature he was simple, entirely free from affectation, with no trace whatever of his being self-conscious of his abilities. He was quite sociable, very polite and considerate to others". – K. Ananda Rao, Professor of Mathematics at Government Arts College in Kumbakonam and later Professor at Presidency College in Madras.

- Ramanujan expressed his gratitude to his mentor Hardy, on his election to the Fellowship of the Royal Society: "My words are inadequate to express my thanks to you. I did not even dream of the possibility of my election" – February 1918.

- "My heartfelt thanks for your kind telegram", wrote Ramanujan to Hardy and that "After your success in getting me elected by the Royal Society, my election at Trinity probably became very much less difficult this year", 1919.

- "Please tell Mr. Littlewood and Major MacMahon that I thanked them very much. Had it not been for your pains and their encouragement, I would be neither the fellow of the one nor that of the other".

- Hardy and Ramanujan discovered an exact formula for the number of partitions of an integer n, p(n), in what has been described by the mathematician Bela Bollobas, in a "Singularly Happy Collaboration.

- … I believe Hardy was not the only mathematician who could have done it. Probably Mordell could have done it. Polya could have done it. I'm sure there are quite a few people who could have played Hardy's role. But Ramanujan's role in that Particular partnership I don't think could have been played at that time by anybody else. … We owe the theorem to a singularly happy collaboration of two men, of quite unlike gifts, in which each contributed the best, most characteristic and most fortunate work that was in him. Ramanujan's genius did have this one worthy of it". — J.E. Littlewood.

- "Ramanujan was a mathematician anxious to get on with the job. And after all I too was a mathematician, and a mathematic- ian meeting Ramanujan had more interesting things to think about than historical research. It seemed ridiculous to worry about how he had found this or that known theorem, when he was showing me half a dozen new ones almost every day." — G.H. Hardy.

- When a truly great like the Hindu Ramanujan arrives unexpectedly out of nowhere, even expert analysts hail him as a gift from Heaven". — E.T. Bell. "An ordinary genius is a fellow that you and I would be just as good as, if we were only many times better. There is no mystery as to how his mind works. Once we understand what he has done, we feel certain that we, too could have done it. It is different with the magicians. They are, to use the mathematical jargon, in the orthogonal complement of where we are and that working of their minds for all intents and purposes incomprehensible. Even after we understand what they have done, the process by which they have done is completely dark." — Marc Kac.

- "Scrolls containing the most complicated mathematics used to unfold before his eyes" and "that Lord Narasimha had appeared to him in a dream and told him that the time had not come for making public the fruits of his research", wrote Ramanujan in a letter to his classmate in Pacchaiyappa's college.

- Ramanujan, like Sir Issac Newton was an unquestioning believer and in the words of E.T. Bell: "A rational mind is sometimes the queerest mixture of rationality and irrationality on earth". – Eric Temple Bell (1883 – 1960).

David Hilbert
(1862 – 1943)

Eric Temple Bell
(1883 – 1960)

Marc Kac
(1914 – 1984)

In a lecture devoted to Ramanujan, G.H. Hardy said:

"I do not believe in the immemorial wisdom of the East, and the picture which I want to present to you is that of a man who had his peculiarities like other distinguished men, but a man in whose society one could take pleasure, with whom one could drint tea and discuss politics or mathematics; the picture in short, not of a wonder from the East, or an inspired idiot, or a psychological fraud, but of a rational human being who happened to be a great mathematician. ...

"... All of Ramanujan's manuscripts passed through my hands, and I edited them very carefully for publication. The earlier ones I wrote completely. I had no share of any kind in the results, except of course when I was actually a collaborator, or when explicit acknowledgement was made. Ramanujan was almost absurdly scrupulous in his desire to acknowledge the slightest help." -- G.H. Hardy, in a footnote on p.xxxiii in "Collected Papers by Srinivasa Ramanujan", Ed. by G.H. Hardy, P.V. Seshu Aiyar and B.M. Wilson, Chelsea, new York (1962).

*Janaki Ramanujan, with foster son W. Narayanan
and the Chairman of the Madras Port Trust,
at a function in honour of Ramanujan.*

G.N. Watson lectured on Ramanujan's Notebooks, in 1931. Watson's Presidential address to the Royal Society, in 1935, was on the mock theta functions of Ramanujan. Facsimile edition of the Notebooks (2 vols.) published, 1957, by the Tata Institute of Fundamental Research. The formidable task of editing the Notebooks started by Bruce C. Berndt with his interest in some theorems of Ramanujan in 1974 . His five Part work entitled "Ramanujan's Notebooks", published by Springer-Verlag ended in 1997. Berndt significantly remarks:

THE JOURNAL
OF THE
Indian Mathematical Society

VI. XII.]   JUNE 1920.   **[No. 3**

THE LATE MR. S. RAMANUJAN, B.A., F.R.S.
BY P. V. SESHU AIYAR.

AS very little is known to the public of the private life of the late Mr. Ramanujan, a few personal details, such as the present writer was privileged to know and learn, may not be out of place in this memorial number of the Journal.

Srinivasa Iyengar Ramanuja Iyengar was born on the 9th day of Margasirsha in the Samvat Sarwajit answering to the English date of 22nd of December 1887, in the house of his maternal grandfather at Erode,—that picturesque spot in South India in whose neighbourhood the Bhavani with overflowing waters meets and combines with the Cauvery. His parentage was humble ; his father and his paternal grand-father were both accountants (literally *gumastas*) to cloth merchants at Kumbakonam, while his mother's father had entered Government service as *amin* in the Munsiff's Court at Erode. His mother, who survives him in great sorrow, is a shrewd and cultured lady, and Ramanujan took his features after her. As is usual with Brahmin boys, he was put to school at the age of five, and before seven he was transferred to the Town High School, Kumbakonam. Even at that early age, he used to puzzle his parents and teachers with questions about zero and imaginary quantities, the distances between the stars and the earth, and the like.

From boyhood, Ramanujan was found to be of a contemplative mood and sedentary in habits ; he seldom associated with his school-mates at play. A correspondent, who was Ramanujan's class-mate at Kumba-

11

The Obituary Notice — in the Journal of the IMS, Vol. VI,
June 1920 — by P.V. Seshu Aiyar.

"The notebooks were originally intended primarily for Ramanujan's own personal use and not for publication ... Some of Ramanujan's incorrect theorems, in number theory found in his letters to Hardy have been well publicized. Thus, perhaps some think that Ramanujan was prone to making mistakes. However, such thinking is erroneous ... Ramanujan's accuracy is amazing."

Ramanujan's work has inspired generations of Mathematicians. The fact that there are three journals named after him - Journal of the Ramanujan Mathematical Society, The Hardy-Ramanujan Journal, and the Ramanujan Journal - and hundreds of papers have appeared and continue to appear based on Ramanujan's work, reveal the enduring nature of his contributions. The Collected Papers of Srinivasa Ramanujan, originally published in 1927 and Ramanujan: Twelve lectures on subjects suggested by his life and work, by Hardy first published in 1940, have both been reprinted in 1999 by the American Mathematical Society. This clearly shows the relevance and importance of the original papers of Ramanujan even today.

The discovery of the 'Lost' Notebook of Ramanujan and its first announcement by George E. Andrews, in the Spring of 1976, and the editing of the Notebooks from 1974 by Byruce C. Berndt contributed to a resurgence of interest in the work of Ramanujan.

During Ramanujan's birth centenary year, 1987, a two-part Video programme on Letters from an Indian Clerk was made by An Independent Communications Association Production for Cannel 4 with WGBH/Boston. In it Ramanujan's Kumbakonam and Hardy's Cambridge are shown with interviews of Profs. Bela Bollobas, a Hungarian Number Theorist at Cambridge; George E. Andrews) the discoverer of the Lost notebook; S. Chandrasekhar, the Astrophysicist who was an admirer of Ramanujan all his life; and C.J. Hamson, Emeritus Professor of Law at the University of Cambrdige, who was then a surviving contemporary of Hardy and Littlewood. This tastefully made documentary (about 55 minutes duration) was produced and directed by the renowned Christopher Sykes. The visuals of Ramanujan were his passport photograph, the photo of his taken after his graduation (wearing a cap and gown) with other graduates, the bust of his made by Paul Granlund. Mrs. Janakiammal was also interviewed and she recalls how Ramanujan was always interested in writing down his 'sums' on paper; that mathematics was everything for him in this universe; and that food was given to him by her by hand while he was writing down his 'sums'; that on his death bed he assured her that whether he is alive or dead, his mathematics would provide for her. It is these pages which he was writing down furiously as he was bed ridden and dying which constitute his 'Lost' Notebook, which is considered by mathematicians today as perhaps the best work Ramanujan did. This is being edited by Bruce Berndt in collaboration with George E. Andrews, Part I appeared in 2005 and Part II in 2008, published by Springer-Verlag.

On the occasion of the 125th Birth Anniversary of Ramanujan, in The Hindu, dated Dec.25, 2011, the following note appeared:

A MISSING BOY: To the Editor of the 'Hindu'

SIR,

Kindly insert the following in your widely circulated journal:

"A Brahmin boy of the Vaishnava (Thengalai) sect, named Ramanujan, of fair complexion and aged about 18 years was till recently a student of the Kumbakonam College. He left his home on some misunderstanding. His guardian is very solicitous about the boy's returning home. He stayed at Rajahmundry for about a month, and was last seen there ve days back. Those who happen to see him are kindly requested to persuade him to return home, and to communicate his whereabouts to: J. SEENIVASA RAGHAVA AYANGAR, 18, Sarangapani Sannidhi Street, Kumbakonam."

This is perhaps the only instance where we have any information about the role of Ramanujan's father in his life. No photograph of the father is available till date!

It is widely believed and reported that the father was least impressed with Ramanujan's extraordinary prowess in Mathematics, and perhaps felt that mathematics will not enable his son to get even a job.

CHAPTER 10

The Indian Science Congress and the π ie Pavilion

The 86th Indian Science Congress was inaugurated by the Prime Minister of India, Rajiv Gandhi, on January 3, 1999 at the Anna University in Chennai. On this occasion, the Chief Minister of Tamilnadu in his speech stated: "Steps have been taken to establish a Ramanujan Museum in the name of the mathematical wizard of Chennai jointly by the University of Madras and the Institute of Mathematical Sciences, here. Mr. Karunanidhi appealed to the Prime Minister to consider 'making the museum into a national asset' ", The Hindu (Jan. 4, 1999).

The idea of developing a π ie Pavilion along with a Ramanujan Museum arose when the author read a half page article in the Mathematical Intelligencer. This idea was made known to a gathering of the relatives of Ramanujan and members of the public at a meeting convened by the Avvai Kalai Kazhagam, on April 26, 1998. Dr. V.S. Ramamurthy, the Secretary of the Department of Science and Technology was the one who said if there is a π Room in Paris, that a π ie (PIE) Pavilion may be created by me for the Indian Science Congress Exhibition and the preceding Childrens Science Congress.

A 12 ft. diameter, 2 ft. deep, wooden, cylindrical structure was designed by the author to display on its inside surface about 404 digits of the transcendental number π. The cylinder made was erected on four wooden pillars at Hall nuber 13 of the Anna University in time for the 6th National Childrens' Science Congress. About 40 laminated Posters were designed. One larger Poster depicted the first 2000 digits of the transcendental number

e. The story of the history of π and e and their relevance in mathematical sciences was illustrated. A poster acquired thanks to the help of Dr. V. Lakshminaryanan of the School of Optometry of the Washington University, St. Louis, Missouri, USA, the monument for e (which the author visited in 1974 on his first visit to that continent) was displayed. of π the two transcendental number which students of mathematics encounter in the conic section formulas and of e which arises in all growth and decay problems, and the complex constant i the constant essential for the transition to quantum mechanics from classical mechanics and the most beautiful equation in the whole of mathematics (according to E.T. Bell):

$$e^{i\pi} + 1 = 0$$

were depicted. The end of the exhibition was with the punch line:

"Never say, $\pi = 22/7$, Never again" !

For, π is a transcendental number (which is <u>not</u> a solution of an algebraic equation like: $x^2 + 1 = 0$ which is an algebraic equation satisfied by $\pm$ i the complex constant).

The Gateway Arch or the Gateway to the West, open to the public from June 1967, is the shape of a catenary, $(e^x + e^{-x})/2 = Cosh\ x.$

- Ramanujan had more creativity than most of the mathematicians. — Bruce Berndt.
- Ramanujan discovered so much and yet left so much more for others in his garden. – Freeman J. Dyson.

Ramanujan was intuition incarnate and one cannot explain how he discovered so many thousands of theorems without any formal education. In Kanigel's book on the Life of Ramanujan, there is a section which has the heading 'Swayambhu'. His incomparable mathematical creativity, with no formal education, will forever remain an enigma, just as the 'big bang' explosion which explains the expanding nature of the our universe is considered as the origin of the universe.

PIE Pavilion and the Ramanujan Gallery. The author explaining the details of the Posters to Dr. V.S. Ramamurthy, DST Secretary & Dr.B.D. Acharya.

A bronze bust of Ramanujan made by the renowned sculptor Paul Granlund to Janaki Ramanujan and the original passport of Ramanujan with her were displayed thanks to the kindness of Mr. W. Narayanan her foster son.

The PIE Pavilion and the Ramanujan Museum (Replica) were fused into the Ramanujan Gallery which is shown above by the author after the ISCE99 and the Gallery were inaugurated by Ms. C.K. Gariyali, I.A.S., the Vice Chairperson of Science City and dedicated to the public at the Periyar Science and technology Center, in Kotturpuram, Chennai, on Science Day, February 28, 1999. The Department of Science and Technology, Government of India, further provided the required funds to set up a Ramanujan Photo Gallery by the side of the Ramanujan Gallery in the PSTC. This Gallery consists of about 120 laminated photographs connected with the life and work of Ramanujan, was completed by the author with the help of Mr. A.T.B. Bose and opened to the public from the end of June 1999.

A decade later, now thanks to the encouragement for the project, initiated by the author, and the efforts of the Excutive Director and the present Vice President of Science City, Dr. Iyamperumal, the Scientific Officer, Dr. Srinivasan and the supporting staff of the PSTC, a floor area of about 2000 sq.ft. is getting ready for a full-fledged Ramanujan Mathematics Museum with exhibits which enable young children to have a hands on experience of mathematical principles. At the higher end details about the origin of the Fields Medal and the 50 Fields Medal winners till date, as well as the Abel Prize winners and the Ramanujan Prize winners, and the citations for their award winning contributions will be exhibited to inspire students of mathematics.

The PIE Pavilion and the Ramanujan Museum. Dr. R. Chidambaram at the Museum. To the right of Dr. Chidambaram are Dr. R. Ramachandran and to his right Dr. B.D. Acharya, besides a few other visitors.

CHAPTER 11

The author has created a website on Ramanujan's life and work during his two-and-a-half year DST funded Project for creating two CD ROMs on the Life and Work of Srinivasa Ramanujan and this website is accessible for all at:

www.imsc.res.in/~rao/ramanujan

The Original Notebooks of Ramanujan and the Collected Papers of Ramanujan can be found at this website (if the access is from a computer which is not fire-walled by the secure system of the Institute of Mathematical Sciences).

Ramanujan: the Man and the Mathematician

In this book of S.R. Ranganathan, published by Asia Publishing House, in 1967, its author reveals his role in the life of Ramanujan:

"In 1923, it was decided that a biography of Ramannujan should be given at the beginning of his Collected Papers. The University of Madras appointed a Committee to write the biography. It consisted of E.M. MacPhail, the Vice-Chancellor, P.V. Seshu Ayyar, Professor of Applied Mathematics in the Presidency College and Secretary of the Indian Mathematical Society, and R. Ramachandra Rao, Education Secretary of the Government of Madras and former President of the Society. As a junior member of the staff of the Department of Mathematics of the Presidency College, it fell to my share to prepare a draft of the biography. As Approved by the Committee, it was published in the Collected Papers in 1927.

"The inaccessibility of this biography in the Collected papers and the ignorance about Ramanujan and his career among University graduates, who had not even heard of his name and whose number

144

had increased considerably between 1950 and 1960, were the motivators for S.R. Ranganathan to write this brief biography entitled: 'Ramanujan the man and the mathematician'."

An All India Radio (Madras) talk on Ramanujan, by Ranganathan, on the occasion of the Platinum jubilee (75th Birthday) of Ramanujan, in 1962, and the response – letters from a couple of the surviving friends of Ramanujan – to that talk, spurred Ranganathan to get reminiscences from all of them, including Janakiammal Ramanujan, over a period of two years.

An anecdote in this book reveals the simplicity of Ramanujan to mundane details, as told by the renowned Indian Statistician, P.C. Mahalanobis, F.R.S., who was a student of King's College, Cambridge, referred to earlier (1913, a year before Ramanujan reached Trinity College): "I was fortunate in forming a good friendship with Ramanujan very soon. It came about in a somewhat strange way. One day, soon after his arrival, I went to see Ramanujan in his room in Trinity College. It had turned quite cold. Ramanujan was sitting very near the fire.

I asked him whether he was quite warm at night. He said that he was feeling the cold though he was sleeping with his overcoat on and was also wrapping himself up in a shawl. I went to his bedroom to see whether he had enough blankets. I found that his bed had a number of blankets but all tucked in tightly, with a bed cover spread over them. He did not know that he should turn back the blankets and get into the bed. The bed cover was loose; he was sleeping under that linen cover with his overcoat and shawl. I showed him how to get under the blankets. He was extremely touched. I believe this was the reason why he was so kind".

Ragami's 'Ganithamedahi Ramanujan' and its translation

In the later half of 1986, I was pleasantly surprised, when Professor E.C.G. Sudarshan, Director of the Institute of Mathematical Sciences, introduced me to Dr. Jasjit Singh, a Railways officer and a writer, who was interested in understanding an article on

Ramanujan, in Tamil. On reading it, I realized that it was a part of a serial and therefore, I requested him to acquire all the articles written in 'Dinamani Kadhir'. due course, he did procure them from the publishers of that newspaper, which had the articles serialized in its weekly edition, from a book entitled "Ganithamedhai Ramanujan", by Mr. T.V. Rangaswami who wrote with the pseudonym Ragami. I translated all the 31 articles of Ragami and sent them to Dr. Jasjit Singh, who wrote a series of four articles in Mathematics Education, a Quarterly Journal of higher education sponsored by the University Grants Commission and published by Macmillan India Limited at that time (but with not even an acknowledgment to the one who translated them for him !).

The second directive was also from Professor Sudarshan who asked me to locate the whereabouts of Janaki the wife of Ramanujan to enable the Hinduja Foundation to honour her on the occasion of the Ramanujan birth centenary. Thanks to the whole hearted support of the Institute authorities, a function was organized on the lawns of IMSc., on April 26, 1986, the Ramanujan Remembrance Day, when a cheque for Rs. 20,000/- was presented by A.P.Venkateswaran, Secretary of the Hinduja Foundation, to Janakiammal Ramanujan and a pension of Rs. 1000/- per mnth was announced, in the august presence of Professor Sudarshan and Dr. V.C. Kulandaisway, Vice Chancellor of the Anna University. The lady, presented to me on April 27, 1986, a copy of Ragami's Tamil book, with her signature on it, which I am preserving and which I used for translating it into English for posterity, as the first attempt at a full-length biography of Ramanujan.

I sought and obtained the written consent and permission of Mrs. Seethalakshmi, widow of Ragami for the publication of an English translation of this book, with the help of my friend Dr. A. Sundaram who accompanied me and helped me in the negotiations with Mrs. Seethalakshmi Rangaswamy. The book is a faithful translation of the original 'Ganithamedhai Ramanujan', without any modifications, published by The Allied Publishers

(Madras) Pvt. Ltd. Ragami had the distinct advantages of being a Tamilian Brahmin, an Iyengar, and a resident of Triplicane where he had plenty of opportunities to come to know and interact with Janakiammal Ramanujan (1899 – April 13, 1994). The traditions of the community were ingrained in his lifestyle and he was able to gather many facts regarding Janaki's association with her illustrious husband from July 14, 1909 when their marriage took place, at Rajendram, till Ramanujan went to Cambridge University on a five year sojourn, 1914 – 1919 and from March 1919 – April 1920, after his return to India.

Since Ramanujan was being treated, unfortunately, for the wrongly diagnosed tuberculosis, for the last thirteen months preceding his premature death. This book was not accessible to a world-side readership of students and admirers of Ramanujan. The author hopes that this will now be read by all who are interested in the life of Ramanujan and its publication also establishes the fact that it is chronologically the first biography (in Tamil) on the life of the mathematical genius.

Busts and a Statue of Ramanujan

Any artist, I believe, would agree that to draw a figure or paint a portrait of a person is not difficult and the quality of the picture would depend on the skills of shading and colouring of the artist. However, to sculpt a bust or a statue of an individual from a two-dimensional photo or portrait depends not only on the skills of the creator but also on his fertile imagination and knowledge of the subject. In the case of Ramanujan, a bust was commissioned almost seven decades after his death, and the sculptors had only an authentic passport photo and the photos of Ramanujan in the ceremonial garb of a graduate or with others in a group. The bust of Ramanujan on the Saraswathi Temple in the Birla Institute of Technology and Science (BITS), Pilani, Rajasthan, is perhaps the earliest sculpted, and the later busts sculpted by Paul Granlund, N. Masilamani and K.G. Ravi are described below.

The challenge of transforming the two-dimensional Passport Photograph of Ramanujan into a three-dimensional bust was taken up by Paul Granlund, Sculptor-in-Residence st athe Gustavus Adolphus College at Saint Peter, Minnesota, U.S.A. A copy of the bust was presented to the Indian Academy of Sciences, Bangalore, by Professor S. Chandrasekhar and Mrs. Lalitha Chandrasekhar. On that occasion, a tribute to Ramanujan from Professor Richard Askey, who played a key role in its commissioning, was read out and this is reproduced here from Patrika, the Newsletter of the Academy, (No. 10, April 1983):

"In the spring of 1976, Andrews went to Europe for a meeting and stopped in Cambridge to see what old manuscripts he could find. One of the finds was not a manuscript but 140 pages of formulas in Ramanujan's handwriting.

"The story of the thread from these sheets to the bust is simple. Andrews has done a lot of very deep work trying to understand what Ramanujan discovered. Eventually, 'The New York Times' heard about it and interviewed him. 'The Hindu' followed with a more extensive interview and also published an interview with Ramanujan's widow, Janki Ammal.

She lamented the fact that a statue of Ramanujan had never been made, although one had been promised. Andrews sent me copies of these interviews, and after a couple of months my subconscious mind finally got through to my conscious mind and it was clear that a bust should be made. Since Janaki Ammal was 80, time was important, so it was up to individuals rather than governments or societies, since institutions move slowly. My first reason for wanting a bust was simple; if the least we could do to show our appreciation of Ramanujan, and while she did not understand his mathematics, she knew that he was one of the few whose work will last. As long people do mathematics, some of Ramanujan's work will be appreciated. Fame is a strange thing and is often fleeting. An interview on a television program is now the accepted form of honour.

"In Ramanujan's case a permanent memorial is appropriate: one which can be appreciated by those who do not understand his mathematics should be added to the memorial Ramanujan made for himself with his work.

"I am pleased to have played a role in this, and would like to thank the more than one hundred mathematicians and scientists who contributed money for the bust which was presented to Janaki Ammal. The bust being dedicated today was donated by a couple who are now friends, Subramanyan and Lalitha Chandrasekhar. When I asked Chandra about the appropriateness of a bust of Ramanujan he immediately replied that it was a good idea and they would do all they could to help. They did. Finally I want to thank the sculptor, Paul Granlund."

Besides the proof copy with the sculptor, ten copies of the bust were made. Two of these castings were acquired by Chandrasekhars and these were gifted by them to the Indian Academy of Sciences and to the Cambridge University.

At present, thanks to the information I have obtained from Professor Askey, we know that five of these busts are in India, two in England and four in the United States of America. The bust presented to Janakiammal is with her foster son W. Narayanan, at the house acquired her – No. 14, Hanumantharayan Koil Street, Triplicane, Chennai. Four other copies are in India, and these are at the Indian Academy of Sciences, Bangalore; the Ministry of Defense of the Government of India, New Delhi; The Tata Institute of Fundamental Research, Mumbai; and The Inter-University Consortium for Astronomy and Astrophysics, Pune. Two copies of the bust are in England, at the Pure Mathematics Library of Cambridge University and at the Royal Society in London. Four other copies are in the USA. Of these, two are with the Gustavus Adolphus College, St. Peter, Minnesota and at the Vaughn Foundation in Houston, Texas.

Ramanujan's busts sculpted by Paul Granlund and by N. Masilamani.

On the occasion of the birth centenary of Srinivasa Ramanujan, on December 22, 1987, Acting Vice Chancellor of the University of Madras, India's first Neuro-Surgeon, Dr. B. Ramamurthy, was requested by me that a fitting memorial should be set up for the 'natural genius' in Madras and an appeal should be made for the artefacts and letters concerning Ramanujan and that they should be preserved along with his Original Notebooks in a Museum. As a consequence, Dr. Ramamurthy, set up a Committee with me included in it as a Member, and he had a Syndicate Resolution passed and he also made a public appeal through the newspapers. This committee got the bust of Ramanujan sculpted by N. Masilamani, who belongs to a hereditary Sthapathigal (sculptor) family.

He was trained in the traditional art of sculpting by his father, who was felicitated by the Government and other agencies for excellence in Arts. This project was executed with the enthusiastic support extended by the Director of the Ramanujan Institute for Advanced Study in Mathematics, Dr. K.S. Padmanabhan and its faculty: Professors M.S. Rangachari, P.S. Rema, G. Rangan, Geetha Srinivasa Rao and others. This bust was unveiled on March 26, 1993, during a Special Symposium on Approximation Theory, convened and conducted by Dr. Geetha Srinivasa Rao, as a part of the Silver Jubilee of the University Grants Commission conferring an Institute for Advanced Study status to the Department of Mathematics of the University and merging it with the Ramanujan Institute founded, in 1950, with Professor C.T. Rajagopal as its Director, by Alagappa Chettiar. This bust is in the foyer of the Ramanujan Institute.

On the occasion of the centenary of the Madras Port Trust, its Chairman, V. Selvaraj, I.A.S., sanctioned to Janakiallal a life-time pension of Rs. 300/- per month. The first monthly pension amount was given to her by the Union Minister of Shipping and Transport, Veerendra Patil, on December 5, 1981. A newly acquired water barge was named as Srinivasa Ramanujan and the Chairman of the Madras Port Trust presented a framed photograph of the ship to Janakiammal on January 6, 1983, at a function. A bust of Ramanujan, sculpted by Mr. Mani Nagappa, was unveiled at the Madras Port Trust, on January 17, 1990 and it is shown below:

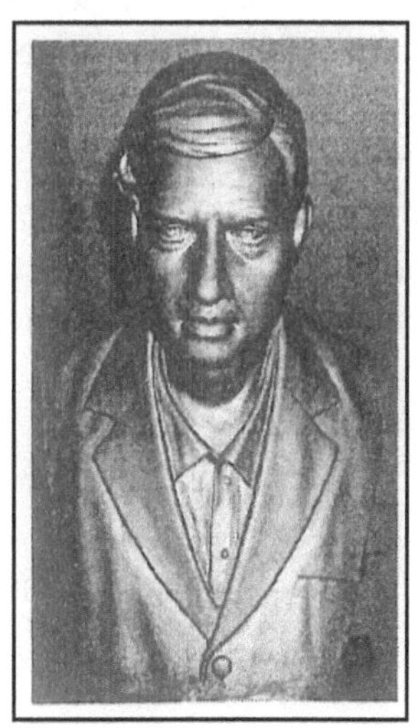

The inscription on the pillar of the bust reads:

Thiru Srinivasa Ramanujan, F.R.S. (London). Born: 22 – 12 – 1887. Died: 26 – 4 – 1920.

An Employee of Madras Port Trust in the year 1912. Bust unveiled by Hon'ble Minister Thiru Murasoli Maran, Minister of Urban Development, in the presence of Thiru K.P. Unni Krishnan, Hon'ble Union Minister of Surface Transport and Communication, on 17th Jan. 1990.

– A. Balraj, I.A.S., Chairman.

Chapter 12

The Wren Library

King's College, Trinity College and St. John's College of Cambridge University are adjacent to each other on Kings Parade, which narrows into Trinity Street. The spacious quadrangle with lush green and velvety lawns behind the picturesque main facades of these Colleges come as a total surprise to any visitor (like me), who would also be greeted by numerous 'PRIVATE', "NO ENTRY' sign boards, warding the visitor off from the premises. These magnificent court yards are open to the public from 12 Noon to 2 P.M. and the visitors are requested to be conscious of the studying atmosphere and the fact athat some of the quadrangles are also residences of these scholars. Hardy and Ramanujan resided in the campus of the Trinity College itself, in rooms opposite to the Wren Library, named after Christopher Wren containing the collections as in 1820s, with later additions. Its internal size is 191 ft. x 40 ft. and is 38ft. high. The four statues on the roof represent Divinity, Law, Physics and Mathematics. This library has a total stock of more than 300,000 volumes of which 2500 early manuscripts (including 1250 medieval, 750 are 15th century printed books), and 75,000 pre-1820 printed books, the Capell collection of Shakespeariana, books from Sir Isaac Newton library, and the Rothschild collection of 18thcentury English literature – a veritable treasure house for the readers.

The Wren Library and Neville's Court.

With the help of Robert A. Rankin, the Ramanujan papers were catalogued and preserved. With an introduction by him to the Librarian of Wren Library the author had access for two days to the archival material in three card board boxes (of about 2" high, foolscap size).

These have the reference addresses as Add.Ms.a.94 with a superscript which refers to the specific document. Details of his card catalogue are with the author and in an article entitled "Ramanujan Papers" (Matheamtics Student, 1997).

In 1980, Professor K. Venkatachaliengar quoted Hardy's remarks to Professor S.R. Ranganathan, in his article "Ramanujan's Manuscripts – II", in Maths Student (vol. 52, 1984, p.215) that 'Ramanujan belongs to your country, the proper place for his Notebooks is your own University Library and added:

"Naturally what applies to Ramanujan's Notebooks applies equally to the other manuscript material which were passed on by Prof. Hardy in subsequent years to Professor Watson. I request our younger colleagues & the Madras University to request the Universities of Oxford and to deliver all the Ramanujan manuscripts to our country keeping Photostat copies of all of them in England. This would naturally take time; hence I request the University College and institutes of higher learning in our country to obtain photostat copies of the manuscripts at Oxford and Cambridge [The cost may be a couple of thousand rupees] and make them available to interested scholars of our country."

In his Presidential Address to the 45th and 46th Conferences of the Indian Mathematical Society, held at Ranchi, in Dec. 1979, and at Bangalore, in 1980, respectively, Prof. K. Venkatachaliengar spoke about the Ramanujan Manuscripts. He ended his 1979 address with the plea:

"The task of getting the originals or at least photo copies of all the manuscripts must be undertaken by our coutrymen, who should also face the formidable task of editing them, taking at first those parts which are comparatively easy to edit; this is true of his elliptic function formulae which Ramanujan has given in nearly half of his Notebooks. ... May I hope that the University Grants Commission will engage scholars to perform this task as early as possible".

The Birth Centenary and the 125th Birth Anniversary have been celebrated. These were inaugurated on the 22nd December 1987 by Shri Rajiv Gandhi, the Prime Minister of India, and by Dr. Manmohan Singh, the present Prime Minister, on December 26, 2012. However, the Ramanujan papers are still to be acquired by this country. The National Board for Higher Mathematics which started celebrating the 125th Birth Anniversary and declared this year as the "2012 Year of Mathematics" hopefully will fulfil this wish of Venkatachaliengar and several other mathematicians who share his view.

Robert Kanigel's acclaimed book: "The Man who knew Inifinity", (Charles Scribner's Sons, New York, 1991; Indian Edition by Rupa & Co. 1994), in 438 pages, has intertwined into a braid three stories: the story of Ramanujan, the inscrutable intellect with a simple heart; the story of G.H. Hardy, Ramanujan's mentor who not only recognized the genius in the 'tattered garb in which he was clothed', but also brought him into limelight; and a silhouette of the mathematical work of Ramanujan and Hardy.

Professor George Andrews released the facsimile edition of the 'Lost' Notbook of Ramanujan on December 22, 1987, with Janakiammal and her family (W. Narayanan is at the extreme right). Robert Rankin and Mrs. Rankin are behind Andrews.

The Ramanujan Museum

In 1962, on the occasion of the 75th birth Anniversary of Ramanujan, P.K. Srinivasan, an ardent, enthusiastic mathematics Teacher at the Muthialpet High School, Madras, started an effort, with courage, conviction, enthusiasm and earnestness, which culminated in the release, in 1968, of "Ramanujan: Letters and Reminiscences" and "Ramanujan: an Inspiration", two Memorial Numbers, containing the first ever collection of letter written by, on behalf of, and to Ramanujan. In an editorial to the first of these two Edited volumes, he wrote about the formation of a "Ramanujan Memorial Foundation, with an object of setting up a permanent memorial to Ramanujan in the shape of a multi- storey building in Madras, housing a plaentariu, mathematics exhibition wings, auditorium, library and show rooms displaying applications of mathematics in Industry. It will be a house of entertainment 'par excellence' for the layman and it will strive to make mathematics as popular as dance and music."

To fufil that dream of his, he had a room set apart as the Ramanujan Museum in the Avvai Kalai Kazhagam (Avvai Academy) in Royapuram, Chennai. This 'museum with a mission' is best described in the words of its Founder (resident) Curator, (late) Mr. P.K. Srinivasan himself:

"Way back in May 1968, when Rajaji released the two volume Ramanujan Memorial Numbers at Gokhale Hall, it was announced that there should be a museum to inspire people with the creative genius of Ramanujan and his singular life of dedication to mathematics. The announcement was received with thunderous applause. Since 1968, all attempts to find a patron for housing the museum did not bear fruit. Nor was any museum started. Avvai Academy, a premier organization founded in 1992 in North Madras with its redoubtable secretary Mr. A.T.B. Bose came forward to give the museum a place as one of its units. On 18th March 1993, the Museum was declared open by our elder statesman Sri C. Subramaniam, who has been awarded the country's highest honour of Bharat Ratna, in Feb. 1998." ...

"With handsome financial assistance of The Hindu, thanks to Mr. N. Ravi, distinguished editor who readily granted the request of the Srinivasa Ramanujan Museum Associates represented by Sri S. Balathandapani of National Law School, a former student of the curator, sixty one custom made commercial art produced, laminated and framed bilingual (Tamil & English) charts of uniform size were procured and placed in the museum in 1995. They contain the jottings of interest to school students – jottings culled by the curator from the Notebooks. This became the second phase. ...

"It is gratifying to note that Prof. C.G. Swaminathan donated in August 1994, one original letter of Ramanujan to his late father Prof. C.N. Ganapathy Iyer of Presidency College. This was an important addition to museum as it tells us where Ramanujan saw Prof. Hardy's book: 'Orders of Infinity' that triggered their correspondence.

"Now we are gathered to witness to this 76th Remembrance Day of Ramanujan a historic event of Mrs. Saraswathi Dole donating to the museum three original letters written by Ramanujan to her late father Mr. E. Vinayaka Row, thanks to the recommendation of Prof. K. Srinivasa Rao of MATSCIENCE. ...

"Attached to the museum an active Math Education Center is functioning to take up the neglected areas of math education such as teacher growth through credit courses in intensive practicals, indigenization of math curriculum through incorporation of Kolam and folk mathematics, interschool primary math Olympiad, help to schools in organizing math club, math lab and math expo, in building up the math section of the libraries and display of wall paintings of mathematical interest, publication of recreational math books and alternative instructions. Culturisation of mathematics through greeting school days with date magic square, magic square dances and inclusion of mathematical themes in school annuals and school dramas, production of math learning kits, summer math camps, reference library for journals, etc."

The stature and achievements of Srinivasa Ramanujan, hailed as one of the greatest Mathematicians of the 20th Century, should be an eternal source of inspiration for students of Science. This can best be achieved through setting up a National Science Museum. Like the Sistine Chapel of the Vatican, pointers in such a Museum should be to the original Notebooks of Ramanujan in its sanctum sanctorum!

Setting up a Science Museum where the emphasis is not on the Technological applications but on the underlying scientific facts and their discovery requires ingenuity, skill and planning, by the best brains of the country. One can take the examples of similar museums in the world like the Deutsches Museum, Munich; the Science Museum, London; the Smithsonian Museums, in USA; and the Pi Room in Paris; and, in India, the Visveswaraya museum in Bangalore and the Museums established in Bangalore, Calcutta and Pilani.

If and when such a National Science Museum is established in India, to popularize and perpetuate the contributions of our Scientists, our Government can approach the British Government for the Original papers of the Natural Genius Ramanujan in the Wren Library. In such a Museum the works of our great scientists – Satyendranath Bose, Sir C.V. Raman, S. Chandrasekhar, should be preserved.

Concluding remarks

In the last letter Ramanujan wrote to Hardy, he did not even hint to Hardy that he had not recovered from his suspected tuberculosis and that his health was on the decline despite the best medical attention bestowed on him by his caring friends and relatives. However, it contained the heart-warming news to Hardy, who strangely did not try to reach him after he left for India, that he had found new result on what Ramanujan called as 'mock' theta functions. In fact, this work of Ramanujan during the last year of his life cannot be described in better words than those of Professor Richard Askey, which are worth repeating again here: "Try to imagine the quality of Ramanujan's mind, one which drove him to work unceasingly while deathly ill and one great enough to grow deeper while his body became weaker. I stand in awe of his accomplishments; understanding is beyond me. We would admire any mathematician whose life's work was half of what Ramanujan found in the last year of his life while he was dying". … When I told Professor Askey that there is only one small change I would like to make in this quotation, which is to replace 'half' [of what Ramanujan did] with 'a fraction' [of what he did], Askey quipped 'half is also a fraction'!

It is an interesting fact that after Dr. S.R. Ranganathan left the University of Madras, he became the Chief Librarian at the Benares Hindu University. It was he who drew the attention of Dr. K. S. Krishnan, the student and collaborator of Sir C.V. Raman, regarding the Notebooks of Ramanujan.

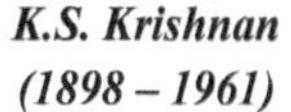

K.S. Krishnan	*Homi J. Bhabha*	*Jawaharlal Nehru*
(1898 – 1961)	*(1909 – 1966)*	*(1889 – 1964)*

At that time, Dr. K. S. Krishnan was a neighbour of Pundit Jawaharlal Nehru in Allahabad and he induced Ranganathan to write to Dr. Homi J. Bhabha at the Tata Institute of Fundamental Research in Bombay. Subsequently, Ranganathan, Krishnan and Bhabha called on Pundit Nehru and as a consequence the facsimile edition of the Notebooks of Ramanujan were published without commentary, which were reprinted in recent times, by the NBHM, on the occasion of the 125th Birth Anniversary of Ramanujan and released by the Prime Minister, Dr. Man Mohan Singh, on December 26, 2011.

An unused cover design for my book on Srinivasa Ramanujan (with my Pencil drawing, 1998) and the stamp issued on the occasion of the 75th Birth Anniversary of Ramanujan (1962).

In fine, the publication of this book has been inspired by the request of Professor P. Jagadeesan, Founder of the Srinivasa Ramanujan Academy of Maths Talent, (98 / 99, Luz Church Road, Mylapore, Chennai – 600004), asking me to write the facts about the life and work of Ramanujan, keeping the mathematical content to a minimum. It is the hope of the author that this effort will provide a first introduction to arouse the interest of the students and the teachers of schools and colleges, as well as students of mathematics, for a further study of the life and work of Ramanujan. The author hopes that some of the readers would seek the originals in libraries and a few would follow the researches on Ramanujan's inspired insights and provide their own proofs of a few of the Entries and even discover new results in mathematics. On this optimistic note, the author urges the mathematics student to start his wanderings through "Ramanujan's Garden" – consisting of his Notebooks and his Collected Papers (see, Appendix) – to locate, admire and enjoy the radiating truth of at least a few of the thousands of beautiful flowers and ripe fruits in his mathematical Garden. May Ramanujan's enigmatic mathematical Entries be an eternal source of inspiration for generations of students of mathematics !

ACKNOWLEDGEMENTS

The photographs are either taken by me, from the websites for Ramanujan or books which are the sources for all Ramanujan followers. On behalf of myself and all the admirers of Ramanujan. I record my salutary tribute to (late) Sri P.K. Srinivasan for his stupendous efforts during 1960s which resulted in most of what we know about Ramanujan.

I express my gratitude and thanks to all my teachers at Schools and Colleges, the Directors, colleagues and friends, and the Institute of Mathematical Sciences, especially to Professor Alladi Ramakrishnan, the founder Director of MATSCIENCE, and my mentor, who took me in as a Research Trainee just a week after my M.Sc. final practical examinations and gave complete academic freedom to evolve my career. Last but not the least, I am grateful to the understanding shown to me by my parents, siblings, wife and sons, who took care of all my needs all the time, with unstinted affection.

Leonhard Euler
China-Dianshan
Sculpture Park

Carl Friedrich
Gauss
Braunschweig,
Germany.

Srinivasa
Ramanujan
SETS Campus,
Taramani, Chennai.

REFERENCES

[1] "Ramanujan: Letters and Reminiscences", Memorial Number, Volume 1, The Muthialpet High School, Number Friends Society Old Boys' Committee, Madras-1, Ed. P.K. Srinivasan (1968).

Note: This is the primary source for all concerned with the Life of Ramanujan and the author is indebted to P.K. Srinivasan and his enthusiasm to talk about 'magic squares' and Ramanujan has been an initial source of inspiration to the author.

[2] K. Srinivasa Rao, "Srinivasa Ramanujan: Kumbakonam to Cambridge", Souvenir 2009 of the Srinivasa Ramanujan Academy of Maths Talent, Chennai – 600004 and published in the Asia Pacific Mathematics Newsletter, Vol. 1, No. 2, (April 2011) p. 1 – 8.

[3] "Collected Papers of Srinivasa Ramanujan", Ed. G.H. Hardy, P.V. Seshu Aiyar and B.M. Wilson, AMS Chelsea Publishing, Am. Math. Soc., Providence, Rhode Island (2000).

[4] G.H. Hardy, "Ramanujan: Twelve Lectures on Subjects Suggested by his Life and Work", AMS Chelsea Publishing, Am. Math. Soc., Providence, Rhode Island (2000).

[5] Bruce C. Berndt and Robert A. Rankin,"Ramanujan: Letters and Commentary", History of Mathematics, Vol. 9, AMS-LMS (1995).

[6] T.V. Rangaswamy, alias 'Ragami', "Ganithamedhai Ramanujan", (in Tamil), Pooram Publications (1985) and its English Translation: "Mathematical Genius Ramanujan", by K. Srinivasa Rao, Allied Publishers Pvt. Ltd. (2008).

[7] K. Srinivasa Rao, "Srinivasa Ramanujan: A Mathematical Genius", East West Books (Madras) Pvt. Ltd. (1998).

Appendix

Publications of S. Ramanujan

1. Some Properties of Bernoulli's numbers
   Journal of the Indian Mathematical Society, 3 (1911) 219 - 234.

2. On Question 330 of Prof. Sanjana
   Journal of the Indian Mathematical Society, 4 (1912) 59 - 61.

3. Note on a set of simultaneous equations
   Journal of the Indian Mathematical Society, 4 (1912) 94 - 96.

4. Irregular numbers
   Journal of the Indian Mathematical Society, 5 (1913) 105 - 106.

5. Squaring the circle
   Journal of the Indian Mathematical Society, 5 (1913) 132.

6. Modular equations and approximations to π
   Quarterly Journal of Mathematics, 45 (1914) 350 - 372.x

7. On the integral $\int_0^X \tan^{-1} t \, dt$
   Journal of the Indian Mathematical Society, 7 (1915) 93 - 96.

8. On the number of divisors of a number
   Journal of the Indian Mathematical Society, 7 (1915) 131 - 133.

9. On the sum of the square roots of the first n natural numbers
   Journal of the Indian Mathematical Society, 7 (1915) 173 - 175.

10. On the product $\prod_{n=0}^{n=\infty} \left[1 + \left(x / (a+nd) \right)^3 \right]$
    Journal of the Indian Mathematical Society, 7 (1915) 209 - 211.

11. Some definite integrals
Messenger of Mathematics, 44 (1915) 10 - 18.

12. Some definite integrals connected with Gauss's sums
Messenger of Mathematics, 44 (1915) 75 - 85.

13. Summation of certain series
Messenger of Mathematics, 44 (1915) 157 - 160.

14. New expressions for Riemann's functions $\chi(s)$ and $\Xi(t)$
Quarterly Journal of Mathematics, 46 (1915) 253 - 260.

15. Highly composite numbers
Proceedings of the London Mathematical Society, 2, 14 (1915) 347 - 409.

16. On certain infinite series
Messenger of Mathematics, 45 (1916) 11 - 15.

17. Some formulae in the analytic theory of numbers
Messenger of Mathematics, 45 (1916) 81 - 84.

18. On certain arithmetical functions
Transactions of the Cambridge Philosophical Society, 22, No.9 (1916) 159 - 184.

19. A series for Euler's constant γ
Messenger of Mathematics, 46 (1917) 73 - 80.

20. On the expression of a number in the form $ax^2+by^2+cz^2+du^2$
Proceedings of the Cambridge Philosophical Society, 19 (1917) 11 - 21.

21. On certain trigonometrical sums and their applications in the theory of numbers
Transactions of the Cambridge Philosophical Society, 22, No. 13 (1918) 259 - 276.

22. Some definite integrals
Proceedings of the London Mathematical Society, 2,17(1918)
Records for 17 January 1918.

23. Some definite integrals
Journal of the Indian Mathematical Society, 11, (1919) 81-87.

24. A proof of Bertrand's postulate
    Journal of the Indian Mathematical Society, 11 (1919) 181 - 182.

25. Some properties of p(n), the number of partitions of n
    Proceedings of the Cambridge Philosophical Society, 19 (1919)
    207 - 210.

26. Proof of certain identities in combinatory analysis
    Proceedings of the Cambridge Philosophical Society, 19, (1919)
    214 - 216.

27. A class of definite integrals
    Quarterly Journal of Mathematics, 48 (1920) 294 - 310.

28. Congruence properties of partitions
    Proceedings of the London Mathematical Society, 2, 18 (1920)
    Records for 13 March 1919.

29. Algebraic relations between certain infinite products
    Proceedings of the London Mathematical Society, 2, 18 (1920)
    Records for 13 March 1919.

30. Congruence properties of partitions
    Mathematische Zeitschrift, 9 (1921) 147 - 153.

Papers written by S. Ramanujan with G.H. Hardy

31. Une formulae asymptotique pour le nombre des partitions de n
    Comptes Rendus, 2 January 1917.

32. Proof that almost all numbers n are composed of about log l
    og n factors
    Proceedings of the London Mathematical Society, 2, 16 (1917)
    Records for 14 December 1916.

33. Asymptotic formulae in combinatory analysis
    Proceedings of the London Mathematical Society, 2, 16 (1917)

34. Records for 1 March 1917.
    Asymptotic formulae for the distribution of integers of various
    types
    Proceedings of the London Mathematical Society, 2, 18 (1920)
    112 -- 132.

35. The normal number of prime factors of a number n\\
    Quarterly Journal of Mathematics, 48 (1917) 76 -- 92.

36. Asymptotic formulae in combinatory analysis
    Proceedings of the London Mathematical Society, 2, 17 (1918)
    75 - 115.

37. On the coefficients in the expansions of certain modular functions
    Proceedings of the Royal Society}, A, {\u 95} (1918) 144 - 155.

These 37 research publications of Ramanujan are reprinted in the 'Collected Papers of Srinivasa Ramanujan', edited by G.H. Hardy, P.V. Seshu Aiyar and B.M. Wilson and published first by the Cambridge University Press (1927) and later by Chelsea (1962). The Questions posed and the Answers provided by Ramanujan, 59 in all, in the Journal of the Indian Mathematical Society follow the research papers in the 'Collected Papers'. Besides the Preface, the editors include two biographical Notices, one by P.V. Seshu Aiyar and R. Ramachandra Rao and another by G.H. Hardy, at the beginning of the 'Collected Papers'. Notes on the research publications and some extracts from Ramanujan's letters to G.H. Hardy are in two Appendices, at the end of the 'Collected Papers'.